HOW TO MEMORIZE

The Science & Art Of Memorizing
& Remembering Everything

HOW TO MEMORIZE

The Science & Art
Of Memorizing &
Remembering Everything

EROL OZVATAN

WWW.PAOLIST.COM

Erol Ozvatan
https://paolist.com

Ordering Information:
Quantity sales. Special discounts are available on quantity purchases by corporations, associations, and others. For details, contact the publisher at the address above.

Printed in the United Kingdom.

Publisher's Cataloguing-in-Publication data
Erol Ozvatan.
Title of the book : How To Memorize | The Science & The Art Of Memorizing Everything / Erol Ozvatan.

ISBN: 9798714627453

10 9 8 7 6 5 4 3 2 1

DEDICATION

This book is dedicated to my dear daughter Ceylan Ozvatan.

Contents

Introduction

This book has been written with the intention of teaching anyone of any age how to memorize in the most simple, easy-to-understand way.

With the advances in technology in recent years making us dependent on machines instead of using our own brain power, memorizing can be difficult for many people.

I believe that our mind is our greatest gift. Education shouldn't stop in school, college or university. It is a lifelong journey. And I know that anyone is capable of training their memory to a high standard with the methods covered in this book.

The techniques contained herein will help you to not only memorize things with ease but will also expand your mind. Your brain is a network full of connections and pathways. Every time the brain learns something new it creates new pathways which actually increase your overall brain power.

You will be amazed at how your brain begins to open up and your focus, concentration and imagination improve with your study and practice of these powerful memory methods.

Thank you for choosing this book, and I hope that it will be a useful tool on your journey to developing an amazing memory!

Part 1

Intro To Mnemonics & Memorizing

- What is a mnemonic?
- What is memorizing?
- How to store the information in our memory?

Part 1
Intro To Mnemonics & Memorizing

What is a mnemonic?

A mnemonic is a tool that helps us to memorize a piece of information, and also reminds us of what we have memorized.

A mnemonic acts as a "Reminder Trigger" or a "Clue Trigger " of what you have memorized so you can remember it by its clue.

We often need a clue as a reminder of something we need to keep in mind or to remember. This is where the use of the mnemonics are awesome!

Simply put; A Mnemonic Reminder or A Clue is something that you already must know before you connect a new data item that you are trying to memorize.

In other words, you are connecting a pair of information data with what you already know and with what you are trying to memorize as a pair-link.

Here is a quick example;

Let's say we want to memorize;
"Pick up some fresh Eggs from the local farm.

Now let's choose a mnemonic clue before you memorize the items.

Let's say you choose your "Car" as the "Mnemonic-Clue-Reminder" as you might be driving to the farm.

Now let's pair-link the reminder and the new information together.

Take a few seconds to Imagine yourself "driving your car to the farm, and filling up the back seat with lots of Huge Eggs".

There you have it. The Car and the Eggs are connected by pair-linking the two together. You have memorized a new information item , the "Eggs" with the item you already know attached, which is your "Car".

You can then do this with many items on your list to memorize them.

This is the basic method of memorizing a piece of information using mnemonics. We'll get into more details about this in the following chapter "The Peg method".

To improve your memory, you need to understand each mnemonic tool and its uses. This will lay the foundation for training your brain, and to memorize anything you need to.

What is memorizing?

Memorizing is storing information within our mind, with the help of mnemonic tools. But where in our mind?

It's been said that the area for memorizing and storing information is "the hippocampus area" of our brain.

How does the brain memorize the information?

The brain itself auto-records information throughout the day with an average of 60.000 thoughts with all the **Actions & Emotions** involved within those thoughts. By default, we record all the events on that day, yesterday, a week ago, or even a few years ago. The habits, regular daily activities, and the responsibilities that we have in our lives are made of all the actions & emotions attached to them. This is "The Working

Memory". Our working memory is always recording everything, short and long term, and it does so with very little effort.

So how does our brain store "New" information we purposefully want to memorize other than normal day to day activities?

The hippocampus area of the brain does not by default memorize or remember new information data that you purposely want to commit to memory.

So in order to memorize new information, we need to ourselves create our own storage area within our mind.

This area can then hold all the new information we want it to. This storage area is as known as "The Memory Palace". We can also create areas used as 'mini-storages within the memory palace to store all kinds of data which we call "A Mini-Palace".

So we now know that we need to create a storage area to memorize new information. Simply because all information has to belong to a space somewhere, and within that space, the new information can be placed and stored.

How to store the information in our memory?

When it comes to our memory, our brains use visualizations, locations and associations. Our 'Memory Palace' utilizes these three things in order to store new information in both our short and long term memory.

The Basic Way To Memorize A Piece Of Information

It s is to mentally prepare;

- A Memory Palace with enough locations and space to store the data you want them to contain.
- A location for each item in your palace. So if you have 10 items to memorize, you'd need 10 locations in your

palace.
- Associate and Convert each piece of information into an image, and mentally place that image into the memory palace.
- Revisit your memory palace's locations to retrieve the information you have placed in them.

Part 2

Memory Training Fundamentals

- Encode & Decode Mentally
- Actions
- Emotions
- Long Term Memory
- Memory Palace
- Plan
- Organize
- Images
- Place
- Actions
- Recall

Part 2
Memory Training Fundamentals

Let's start with the fundamentals to give you a better idea of how to memorize almost anything you like at any time you like.

These are the basics path to follow when memorizing a piece of data, whatever the data may be. Simply put, by following this simple formula, anyone can memorize and recall whatever they decide to either keep it a short or a long term data.

Make A Decision To Memorize It If You Want To Remember It

Memorisation takes place in the mind. Everything you want to memorize using the methods taught in improving memory, will be memorized using your mind, and your mind's eye.

This is at its most basic, and it is that you first have to decide to memorize whatever it is you want to memorize so that you can remember whatever it is you want to remember. You cannot remember anything if you have not memorized it already.

If something has not happened, you would not have a recollection of it. There would be nothing to remember.

On the other hand, you'd remember many of the actions you were involved in during your day of activities. You would have the ability to think mentally and picture of your day, all the things that have happened, and the conversations you had with people, and everything else in between.

So this is the same path to follow when you want to memorize anything you like. You first need to decide to memorize it, so you can remember it later. No surprises here. You would convert whatever you like to memorize into a quick movie using the power of your imagination with your mind's eye.

Let see how..

How Our Brain Memorize & Remember

Encode & Decode Mentally

At it's basic, we encode the data to memorize it, and decode the same data to recall it.

Encoding: By mentally converting every single data into an image, adding actions and emotions to strengthen the data, and by placing those images on a familiar route. Simply imagining all of those images on that route in your mind's eye.

Decoding: Mentally walking the same route, and convert them back to data again. Again, imagining all of those images on that same route in your mind's eye.

Actions

Actions are what happens during your day. Many events happens, and each might be different than another, but your brain records it like a movie. This is because you collect all of that data and you by default convert your day into moving images without any force. Just like watching a movie, you remember it all because you can mentally see it as a movie. This is how our brain memorize and remember a piece of information. Our brain sees it all as pictures, and the actions that happens in those pictures.

Emotions

When I first learned about how our brain store the information, I couldn't believe how well it worked even though I thought it was a little silly, but funny at the same time. When I said "a little silly", I never knew that "absurdity" was the key to memorize almost anything! It was a shock, but worked like magic.

Along with absurdity, funny, sad, violence also works really well too.

Simply put, when you mentally memorize a piece of information, think of how it would look like if there was something funny about it, or sadness about it, violence, or even absurdity at its most stupid. Adding emotions to your actions will strengthen the neurons in your brain, and you'll have it memorized and remember with ease. Sometimes you may find that it's almost not easy to forget! This is of course good for long term memory.

Long Term Memory

This is where you'd store different subjects for different interests. To store the data in your brain for a long term, you'd have to use a memory palace for each of your subject.

Memory Palace

This is known as "MoI", or "The Method Of Loci". When you mentally memorize a piece of information, this is where you store it, in a memory palace.

What do we mean by a memory palace?

A memory palace is a palace you know well like your home, or school, or your office, car park, and other places that has rooms in them. It's basically a building with rooms just like homes and offices. And you use that palace as a mental location, so that you can put those images around that palace to memorize your information.

Let's say we have a pin number of "1920" we'd like to memorize for ABC Bank.

We would convert 19 into an image, 20 into another image, add actions and emotions, and then place that final little movie in the front of the entry door at ABC Bank. In its basic that's exactly how easy it is to do. You'd mentally connect an image for 19, image for 20 by adding actions with emotions with the images, and simply see the whole thing mentally happening at that location.

Home as your first memory palace

A quick and often very useful memory palace to start with is your home. Start with your bedroom, bathroom, kitchen, living room, hallway. This is a Five-Room-Palace.

In each room, stand at the door, and choose another five spots. Start with the bedroom, point your finger to the very first spot and say "One", then point on the next spot, and say "Two", point to the next and say "Four", and point your finger to the last spot and say "Five".

So on your first recall location, there may be the "bed" there, your second location may hold a "bedside table", your third a "Mirror", forth a "Chair", fifth a "Bag".

So now you can go back and notice all the furniture, and now call as "One – Bed", "Two – Table" etc until all five locations and the items on those locations are learned.

So now your first room has five other spots. These five spots are "The Recall Locations". And on those locations, make a mental note of all the item there. With five rooms and five locations in each, it would mean you have a Five-Rooms-Palace with a total of 25 Locations. When you need to memorize more long terms information, you'll need to build more palaces. Many easy methods are available to build more palaces with ease. When you build more palaces, just make sure to create a list of them alphabetically so it's easier to memorize and remember!

POIPAR: The Formula To Memorize Anything

So let's see how we memorize any kind of information using the simple formula below.

Plan | Organize | Images | Place | Actions | Recall

The formula here is what we do before, during and after we memorize. It follows a path, so you can plan to make a start, and end it in a Recall whenever you have the need to recall.

So let's dive into what each one is in the order.

Plan

Let's say we want to memorize the details of a new person we have just met, and we want to memorize their name and phone number, and their job title.

The way you plan it out is to think of how many details we need to memorize first as a list;

Name: Mark
Job Title: Banker
Phone: 01 23 45 67 89

So we have "Mark", "Banker", "01 23 45 67 89" with a 10 digit phone number.

Organize

we would need an image for "Mark", and image for Banker, and five images for the phone number. It would also mean that we would need a memory palace with at least 6 locations, 1 for the name and job title, and five spots for the phone number.

Images

Let's now find the images we need to encode the data, so we can memorize it easily.

Mark: Think of this person with a "Huge Check-Mark" on his forehead.

Banker: Think of him counting dollar bills to you at your local bank.

Now lets find the images for the number digits. We'll use the images from the Shaper System.

01: A Spear
23: Swan
45: Chair
67: Hangman Rope
89: Snorkel

Place

This is your memory palace. We will place the data into the locations in your palace.

Let's say this palace is the building of your local bank. And you have chosen 6 locations within it, and know the locations inside out.

We will place all 6 data into the 6 locations we have at the bank.

Actions

On your first location at the bank, think of Mark with a Check-Mark on his forehead, Counting out money to you at the bank's counter. This is known as Pair-Linking a Person. We have linked the Mark as a Banker using a single location. When we pair-link, we connect the first and the second together by an action.

Actions make images move. Simply put, you mentally imagine that the person Mark literally has a Check Mark on his forehead. Closing your eyes while imagining wil help form the images.

On your next 5 locations;

Simply place the "Spear" on the first spot mentally. To strengthen this image add actions and emotions. Think of yourself in the scene, and that you have the spear in your hand, and attacking the banker.

Place the "Swan" on the next location. To strengthen this image add actions and emotions.
Be in the scene, Have the Swan pecking into your leg while at that location. Close your eyes, and imagine this happening with your mind's eye.

Repeat this process with all the rest of the images. And there you have it. You have just memorized all the data.

Adding **actions with a forced emotion will strengthen the whole animated image**. What you are doing is creating a mini scene, just like a movie scene. This is what our brain remembers. Our brain remember animated images, actions and emotions that happens when they are a pair or chain linked together, which creates the little scenes, or mini-stories that are memorable.

Also note: When you build a memory palace, make sure to learn all the items such as the furniture and other items, so that you can use them as "Recall Triggers" as well as "Action Triggers.

Recall Locations: This is the spot where you store your data.

Recall Triggers: These are the items that are already at the recall locations.

Action Triggers: These items are used as "Pegs to create a "Pair-Link" between the data we want to memorize and the item at the location by simply adding an Action & Emotion

Recall

Now is the time to "Revisit The Palace Mentally"

This is where we Encode the data back to its original.

Simply close your eyes, and go to your first location at your local bank.
Who do you see? Mark. Yes. He also still has a Check-Mark on his forehead

Go to the next location, what do you see? You see yourself attacking the banker with a spear, you already know that translates to "01".

Go to the next location, what do you see? You see yourself being pecked by a Swan, you already know that translates to "23".

And so on with the rest of the locations.

So now you can remember Mark, his phone number, and his job Title using a few locations in your memory palace.

Let's now move on to the tools you need to master to memorize everything with limitless possibilities!

Part 3
Twelve Mnemonic Tools
You Need To Master

- Storage & Retrieval: MEMORY PALACE
- The PEG System & The Peg Method
- Acronyms
- Acrostics
- Chunking
- Grouping & Organizing
- Linking Mastery
- Number Shapes
- Number Rhymes
- Story Method
- Visualizing & Imagination
- Spaced Repetition

Part 3
Twelve Mnemonic Tools
You Need To Master

Here are The Twelve Mnemonic Tools & Methods You Need To Master To Memorize Everything

These tools will give you many ideas, insights, techniques and methods that you can use immediately to memorize a list of items, facts, numbers, words, names, procedures, and even a speech! The possibilities are limitless.

1. Storage & Retrieval: MEMORY PALACE

A Memory Palace is a "Mental Storage Space" to save the information you want to memorize, and to retrieve the information once it's memorized. This is mostly how we memorize information either short or long term.

A Memory Palace can be any building, as long as there are multiple locations within that building. When you have chosen a building that you want to use as a Memory Palace, **Make sure to Memorize Your Memory Palace** as all memorisation takes place in your mind.

Once you have those locations in your memory palace, you simply place the information you want to memorize into each location by way of the following available **choices**;

- Simply place the information item into that location.
- Using an existing item in a location, pair-Link the existing item with the information you want to memorize.
- Pair Linking two items together and placing them into the location.
- Chain-Linking a few items together at the location.

A Memory palace has to be pre-organized, based on what you want to memorize.

All memorisation takes place in your mind. You store the information, and you recall the information, all within your mind.

To help you to do this, we use a Memory Palace. We store the information in a memory palace, and all we have to do is to walk back mentally to see what's in there!

A Memory Palace is also known as "The Method Of Loci", or "The Journey Method" which suggests a path to walk through a palace mentally - a building you know well.

The Method Of Using Your Memory Palace

- Choose a building such as your home.
- Choose the rooms in your building
- Choose the trigger Locations
- A finally choose the Items within those rooms

How To Set Up Your "Memory Palace Storage"

So, now we know all about our memory palace and its function, let's get cracking!

* Choose a place that you know very well such as your Home, office, school, bank etc..

- Walk through all the rooms, get to know each room inside out.
- Identify 5 rooms/locations that will hold 5 different items within each room.
- Remember that each 5 items in each room will be your "Permanent Items".
- Commit all the rooms into your mind. Memorize your palace!

- Walk through your palace mentally over and over until it's firmly ingrained in your mind.
- Make sure to mentally *see* all 5 items in each location for each room.
- Count out loud the first 5 items in the first room by pointing your index finger to each item. So when you are standing at the entry of the room, you would count out loud and say "1-Bed" pointing your index finger, then say 2-Table, 3- Mirror, 4-Chair, 5-Shoes. This would be in your first room.
- Memorize your first room with all 5 stops, and the 5 items at those stops.
- Go to the next room, again count out loud 6-Monitor, 7-Bookshelf, 8-Small-Bin, 9- Glasses, 10-Bag. So your second room holds the locations and the items from 6-10.
- Repeat this process for all the rooms in your memory palace. So If you have 5 rooms, your last count would be 25-and-the-item-name.
- Keep a written copy of the memory palace. Draw and/or write it down and store it away.
- Use spaced repetition to revisit the palace from your written copy, repeat the walk mentally.

2. The PEG System & The Peg Method

The peg method is an alternative method for a memory palace. It's a quick way of memorizing a short-list of items attached or hooked with a pair-link to the items known as pegs.

The peg method works by pre-memorized items that are used as hooks to attach the new information by way of pair linking an action between the two.

Remember you have paired a link between your "Car" and "Eggs" earlier?

What you have done is Pair-Linked a Peg item which is your

"Car" which is the item that is pre-memorized, with the new item "Eggs".

That's basically what the peg method is. You attach new information to an item that you already know as a Pair-Link.

The peg method is also a very powerful method for memorizing a list of items that really don't have the need for a memory palace. Although using a memory palace with your paired-peg-links will strengthen the scene and be more memorable, the peg method does not rely or depend on a memory palace so you can memorize your list without the need of creating one.

A peg can be any tangible item. A peg can be your hands, your car, your TV. It can be any item that you have as a list that can be used to attach new information.

Popular Peg List

Use the peg list ideas below to prepare yourself to memorize any short or long list of items.

Find images for each list. Practice memorizing your lists. And use them whenever you have a list of information you want to memorize, without the need of a memory palace. It'll be worth it!

The Peg Palace

Here are some Peg-List ideas you can use for your Peg-Palace.

Alphabet Pegs. A-Z Each with 26 Items Or Pegs.

26 Items Per Alphabet Pegs. With each letter representing a tangible item. Such as;

- **Alphabet Animals**: Animals that start with letters of the alphabet.
- **Alphabet Fruits**: Fruit names that starts with each letter. A: Apple B: Banana.
- **Alphabet NATO:** A: Alpha, B: Bravo, C: Charlie ..
- **Alphabet Persons:** Person names that starts with alphabet letters.
- **Alphabet Shapes.** Items that look like the objects.
- **Alphabet Sounds:** A-Ape, B-Bee, C-Sea..

A Total of 156 Alphabet pegs.

- **Number Digit Pegs**
  Basic 0-9 Number shapes. Gives 10 items you can use as hooks or pegs.
- **Number Rhymes Pegs:** I have listed 30 Items you can use as pegs.
- **The Shaper System Images** as Pegs from 00-99. Gives you 100 Pegs!
- **Major System Pegs** 00-99: Items that are made of

words using the phonetic sounds. 100 Pegs.
A Total of 240 Number-Digit pegs.

Everyday Object Pegs

- **Colour Pegs**: 10 Pegs. Choose 10 Colours and use them as pegs. Such as "Red-Car" as a Pair-Link. You can simply use the colours to link with your list with whatever you want to memorize.
- **Musical Instruments:** Choose 10 musical instruments, find images you can use which will give you another 10 pegs.
- **School Items:** Choose 10 items that you would take with you if you went to a school, find images you can use which will give you 10 pegs
- **Planets:** If you have memorized all 10 planets already, why not use them as the next 10 pegs.
- **Market/s**: Choose 10 items that you always buy which gives you 10 more pegs.
- **Car**: Choose 10 item-spots around your favorite car. Gives you 10 more pegs.
- **Office**: Choose at least 10 office items. 10 more pegs.

A Total of 70 Everyday Objects pegs.

Persons & Body Pegs

Your Body: Choose 10 spots on your body
and you have another 10 pegs, such as;

Hair | Eyes | Nose | Mouth | Chin

Neck | Chest | Stomach | Legs | Feet.

Simply use the areas of the body, and pair-link your data with each part of the body.

Other People's Body

Remember you have a list of 26 people in alphabetical order? Why not use each body with 10 spots as above? Perhaps you may even use their unique clothing as pegs as well. And you have another 260 pegs!

A Grand Total Of: 736 Pegs for your Peg-Palace!

Using Pegs with the linking method

With the linking method, we use the pegs with;

- Familiar (pegs) + Familiar (pegs) such as memorizing number digits.
- Familiar + Unfamiliar (not pre-memorized and new) such as attaching words/objects.
- Unfamiliar + Unfamiliar, two items not pre-memorized pair-linked by an action.

One of the examples for Familiar + Unfamiliar is learning a foreign word where we attach an unknown word to a known word.

With the Link method, we can use pegs and apply an action involving the two, or more. We can use pre-memorized pegs, and/or unfamiliar objects with other objects, which can then be either attached to a pre-memorized peg, or at a spot in your memory palace.

I mostly use the memory palace method, because even if I use the peg system, I still have to place the linked image onto a location, and the scene becomes much more memorable.

However, the peg method is great for a short and/or a long list of information and can be used at any time and for any situation. Simply pair link your pegs with the images that represent the information you want to memorize.

Many stage performers use the Peg Method to memorize their speeches, jokes, stories, facts and other data as it's still a very popular and easy method.

It's worth mastering this brilliant mnemonic tool.

Pegs For Short Term Memory

Reusing your pegs on the same hour or the same day may give you ghost images. I would not use the same pegs twice in a day for two different lists.

Wait at least a day before you use the same pegs again for your next list of items.

A to-do list, shopping list, or any daily list can be memorized using the same pegs every day.

You can memorize a few different lists using a few different Peg-Lists every day.

So you might have a To-Do list, Shopping-List, Work-List.

Simply assign a Peg-List to each one of your lists.
And memorize your new list of items using the same peg list every day.

I have 50 items in my little office I use as pegs. I memorized them in a numbered order, so I can go from the first item to the next without any confusion. I memorize a huge list, or a few different lists when I split it into the amount of locations I need each day.

So in a way my office is another memory palace made up of 50 pegs. That's how I construct my memory palaces. I always use the objects that are already in there, or I simply mentally place them there myself.

Pegs for long term memory

You can still use your Peg-List for long term memory. It would just mean that you cannot reuse those pegs again, because you would have your information linked to those pegs permanently. So your pegs become permanent pegs, and so does the info attached to those pegs. I use number shapes, alphabet objects, my body, my-car, musical instruments, office items, and some other everyday objects as Pegs-Storage.

No need to create a memory palace storage if you have a good few Peg-Lists. The idea would be to create more Peg-Lists if you have a lot of long term information you want to memorize.

A Memory palace is always your best friend for <u>long term</u> memory. As mentioned before, I still use my memory palaces to place my pegs along the journey. It becomes an expandable palace. It becomes very memorable, it's almost impossible to forget!

3. Acronyms

An Acronym is a word or made up word that is made of the first letter of other words.

Acronyms help us remember a list of words compressed into a single word.

Here are some examples;

JPEG: **J**oint **P**hotographic **E**xperts **G**roup

NATO: **N**orth **A**tlantic **T**reaty **O**rganization

BBC: **B**ritish **B**roadcasting **C**orporation

ROY G BIV
Red **O**range **Y**ellow **G**reen **B**lue **I**ndigo **V**iolet (Rainbow Colours)

Many public speakers use this simple acronym model to give speeches for an hour or even longer. Here is an example;

SUCCESS: **S**ee your goal | **U**nderstand the obstacles | **C**reate a positive mental picture | **C**lear your mind of self doubt | **E**mbrace the challenge | **S**tay on track | **S**hake The World.

4. Acrostics

Acrostics are words that form a sentence like phrases or quotes, or poems. It's almost the same as an acronym, we still use the first letter of each words, except we create words in replacement of the original list of words.

Here are some examples;

The Order Of The Planets In The Solar System

Original Words:
Sun | Mercury | Venus | Earth | Mars | Jupiter | Saturn | Uranus | Neptune | Pluto

Acrostic Words:
See My Very Easy Method Just Speeds Up Naming Planets

The Order Of Algebraic Equations

Original Words:
Parenthesis | **E**xponents | **M**ultiplication | **D**ivision | **A**ddition | **S**ubtraction

Acrostic Words: (PEMDAS)
"**P**lease **E**xcuse **M**y **D**irty **A**unt **S**andra"

Acrostics For Simple Formulas.

Simply find and use an image for each Symbol & Letter for all

your formulas, and pair or chain link them together as usual into
a mini-story!

D = V * T
Distance = **T**ime * **V**elocity

Imagine Danny **De Vi To** watching a huge **TV** from a distance
in your classroom on the blackboard in your math class.

5. Chunking

Try memorizing this; 2158956970
Or this; tbghsytdpy

Not easy for most people. However, if I now separate them into
two part chunks this is what we would get instead.

Now try it again: 21 58 95 69 70
And this one: tb gh sy td py

Would you agree that the second ones are easier to see, read, and
remember?

That's exactly what chunking is. We separate the data into
smaller chunks because our brain can handle it much better
in **bite size pieces**. And we use those chunks to either pair link,
or chain link them together to create a memorable story,
mentally placed on our memory palaces.

For example; When we memorize numbers, it's much easier to
divide them into two or three digit chunks such as "00 15" , or
"125 895".

Make sure to always chunk your information into smaller parts
each time you want to memorize a list.

6. Grouping & Organizing

If you have a lot of "random" information to memorize, then you may need to organize them into smaller groups.

For example you can separate your clothing lists, shopping lists and to-do lists, so they are all in their own group lists.

You can also group categories into their own groups.

Organizing the outline of any list will help you plan your memory palace and the amount of locations needed within your palace.

Always take your time to think of the systems and the methods you will use first. Next, choose or create a new palace for it with enough locations.

The rest will be to simply practice attaching the information to your memory palace.

7. Linking Mastery

"PAIR" AND "CHAIN LINKING" & Top 5 Methods Of Link-Actions!

PAIR LINKING: We remember better when we connect one piece of information with another piece of information. This is known as a "Pair-Link". We link one item with another to make a connection between the two.

When we Pair-Link two items together mentally, we create a mini-story or a scene from the outcome of the link. These links could be objects and objects, Persons & Persons, or a person and an object. It can be any type of link as long as you can link both together via a story.

CHAIN LINKING

You have probably guessed it already. Chain-Linking is connecting more than two items one after another. So if you have a list of 10 items to memorize, you can easily connect them together by creating a **continuous story**.

And you would of course again make this happen on a location within your memory palace if you want this to be in your long term memory.

Here is an example for "**Pair-Linking and Chain-Linking**" by also using the "**Mini Story Method**" with a starting location on a memory palace;

Let's say we want to memorize this "To-Do List".

9 am: Buy Fuel for the car
10 am: Call Dad
11 am: Library
12 pm: Pay the bill
13 pm: Swim
14 pm: Pick up groceries
15 pm: Car Wash

Let's start with the **location first.**

Since this list starts with buying fuel for the car,
we can **think of the starting location as "The local Fuel Station"**.

* Now imagine you are;

"at the fuel station", and you are "fueling your car", and your "dad calls you on your phone".

You have just Pair-Linked "Fuel & Dad" together.

Location: at the fuel station

First Item in the pair: <u>fueling your car</u>
Second Item in the pair: <u>dad calls you on your phone</u>

Now Let's Chain-Link Them Together By Adding The Time Element to the list.

To remind you of the time which 9 am & 10 am are for both links;

The first way is to use number shape images as pegs-storage, so we can also link them into the story.

The number digit "9" is the shape of a Balloon, number "10" is a "Stick & Drum"

So now we use a "Balloon" and "Stick & Drum" as a peg-storage to remind us of the time as well as the mini-story paired-link for "Fuel & Dad".

Now the story changes into "Location" + "Time-Link" + "Chain-Link" = Mini-Story.

"You are at "The Local Fuel Station" + "A Balloon is tied on the fuel cap" and "you open cap with the balloon stuck to it, and start <u>fueling your car</u>" and your "<u>dad calls you on your camera phone</u>" wearing a "Huge Drum Stuck On His Head''.

You have now created a Chain-Link and produced a "Mini-Story" using a memory palace location, and a peg to store the time.

Let's analyze the chain-link here;

You have used a single location, and placed a chain-linked mini-story for the first Two-Items with their corresponding times.

Location: <u>at the fuel station</u>

First Item in the pair: <u>fueling your car</u>
First Peg-Storage Item: Balloon for digit number "9"
Second Item in the pair: <u>dad calls you on your phone</u>
Second Peg-Storage Item: Drum for digit number "10"

This is exactly how we mentally pair and chain link to create a mini-story, and store them at the mental location we have chosen, either on the spot, or at a pre-memorized memory palace.

Person Object Paired-Link

One other way to memorize this is to use PO: Persons, Objects, and action-links.

Let's say you have 100 people from 00-99.

Your 09 would be a person who would represent "09 am".

Let's say your 09 Person was Superman;

Your story would look something like this;

"Superman is at The Local Fuel Station, Fuelling The car, while talking to his Dad on the phone who is wearing a huge drum on his head".

Location: Fuel Station: **"Memory Palace"**
09 am: Superman: **"Person"**
Fuelling The Car: 2 Items or **"Objects"**
Pair-linked: by an **"Action"** -> "While talking to his Dad on the phone" "who is wearing a huge drum on his head."

It takes a lot of lines of text to explain how the whole thing works, but as you can see it's just a matter of practice to memorize all of this information within a matter of a few seconds at a time.

When you practice these skills, you'll notice yourself getting better and faster at creating pair and chain links, and having lots of fun with it!

Now let's move on to the rest of the list by chain-linking them together to give you some more ideas;

When your Dad calls you, he tells you that he is waiting for you at the local library. Now you have just linked "Library" to "Dad" which creates the first chain-link.

Now we will connect the Library to 'Bills' to continue with the chain-linking.

You arrive at the library, go to the desk, and Pay the bill to the Librarian at the desk. Imagine yourself walking in and immediately paying the bill at the reception inside the library.

Let's now connect "Bills" with "Swimming".
As you pay the bill, you notice the library's floor is flooded with water rising up to chest level. You start "Swimming" out from the building.

Let's now connect "Swimming" with "Groceries".

As you swim out of the library building, you notice a lot of groceries floating around, and you simply pick them up and bag them up.

Let's now connect "Groceries" with "Car-Wash".

Let's go crazy this time, and let's wash the car with the groceries you have just picked up!

As you can see, you simply connect two items together, and then create the next 2 by using the previous and next by chain-linking them together.

And by doing so, you are creating a crazy story that may just take you a couple of minutes to think and to mentally visualise, but will stay with you for the rest of the day!

As for connecting the times with your To-Do List, or any list, you would need a number system as explained above, so that you can also connect them into your Paired-and-Chained-Links.

There are a few "Number To Image Generator" systems. I use The Shaper System as my own number to image generation which are all pre-made so it's always available to use as and when I have the need to.

Pair-Linking with Memory Palace Only

You can also use the same list to memorize without a chain-link. This is where we use a memory palace for all the paired links.

Here's how you'd do it using one of your "**Memory Palace Storages**".

Choose a memory palace. Pair-Link the first 2 items together with Fuel & Dad, and place that scene onto the first Trigger

Location in your memory palace.

Next you pair-link "Library & Bills" and place that onto the next Trigger Location in your memory palace.

And repeat this process with as many paired-links as needed! Use pegs-storage items where necessary inside your memory palace.

Top 5 Action-Methods Of Pair-Linking and Chain Linking!

If put into practice, following these tips, methods and insights will ensure you'll never run out of actions and imagination!

When we pair link two bits of information, we create actions between the first and the second item by way of our imagination.

However, it's not always easy to find an action when we link items together such as "Toothbrush" and "Spaceship". They have no logical connection to each other. It can be a struggle to find an action to link them together.

This is where the top 5 methods of linking come in handy to learn, remember, and to apply.

1. "Mini & Mighty" Link Method

This is where you make your objects mentally shrink or enlarge by way of an action. It's a very fast method to apply. Read on…

Let's pair link these 2 items for our example;

"Airplane" & "Pen".

<u>A quick reminder of Words to Images System</u>
Each time you have words, associate and convert them into images. And each time you convert them into images, go through the questions below;

- What type of object is it? What type of Airplane is it? * What does it look like? What does this type of airplane look like?
- What does it sound like? What sound does it make when it works or does something?
- What does it remind you of? Does it remind you of another object, person, place?
- What colour is it? Is it one colour? Or a few different colours?
- What size is it? How big would you say this Airplane is?

Now do the same with the Pen. Let's now do our example of Shrink Or Enlarge or "Mini" & Mighty" using the two items to pair-link them.

Imagine looking out of your kitchen window, and seeing a Mighty Big Airplane flying towards you, and it gets smaller and smaller, and fits through the window, and lands on your table in the kitchen. And on the table you have this Huge Pen as big as the Table. You pick up the huge pen, and push the length of it through the airplane. It looks like a Pen with Airplane wings!

Mentally shrink the item into a "Mini-Object", and where necessary, make the item the "Mighty Big Object".

This will immediately give you the size to work with your actions.

2. "Morphing & Transforming" Link Method

This is where you make your objects mentally morph or transform into another object. So it becomes the object.

It's also a very fast method to apply. Read on…

Let's go back to the "Airplane", and "Pen" example to do this.

Remember the pen was pushed through the airplane? And it looked like a Pen with Airplane Wings?

Here we have already applied a part of the transforming method to the airplane.

To fully apply this method, you would first start with the Airplane on your table, and then mentally turn into the Pen. So you end up with the Pen as the last object.

But the story would always stick as the transforming method is also a powerful Pair-Linking Tool.

3. "The Multiplier" Link Method

This is where you make your objects mentally multiply in 100s, one after another. Make them come out in many multiples. Let them fly, drop, hit things and add other actions.

It's one of the most fastest & effective methods to apply.

4. "The Superhero Powers" Link Method

This is where you make your Objects or People have Superhero Powers!

 It works great as it is easy, fun and fast to apply.

Let's take the number digits for "46" which is the "Seahorse" in the shaper system.

Now a Seahorse doesn't really give us much to work with as its natural move is very basic. So here we can give him a Superhero Power to have either a set action, or simply give him a quick action for fast and easy memorisation.

Now imagine A Seahorse that has the power of Superman with Laser-Eyes! It Laser Burns everything in front of it!

How many Superheroes with their individual powers do you know? Make a list of all of those powers, and memorize them. Use them when you pair-link your objects, or persons.

5. "The Clue-Shape" Link Method

This is where you "Add your Objects A Clue" so that it would act as another reminder that can be recognised instantly. It works tremendously.

This method requires a pre-memorized list of clues.

Add any type of clue possible. Use Colours, Shapes, Images, Pegs, Logos, Signs, Anything that would remind you of the item, or the next paired item in the list.

**Adding Actions To Your Objects
& Your Persons for PA or PAO.**

Here is A list of Premade Actions you can use to create your Pair, and Chain-Links.

acting	bends (object)	checks
animating	bends (over)	chooses
attacking	bicep curls	clacks
arm-wrestling	biting	climbs
applauding	bounces	comes
asking	bowing	commands
blinking	borrowing	conducts
blowing	breathing	conjures
baking	builds	cooks
balancing	burns	coughs
balancing (self)	burps	cracks
bandages	buys	crashes
bangs	calculating	crosses
barking	carving	crushes
bathing	carries	crying
begging	chases	cuts

dances	feeds	hides
dancing	fights	hitting
delivers	fist pump	holding
digging	flying	holds
dives	flips	howls
draws	flirting	hugs
dreams	floats	hyperventilates
drinks	flying	identifies
driving	gazes	inspecting
drools	give	into
drops	goes	jails
dunk	goes into labour	juggling
eating	grabs	jump shot
electrocute	gurgles	jumping over
enlarges	glued	jumps
explodes	halts	kicking
faints	handstands	kicks
falls	hangs	kisses
farting	harpoons	kissing
faxes	hiccups	knocks

laughs

levitates

licking

licks

limps

lunges

makes

marches

meditates

milks

mixes

moonwalks

mouth to mouth

nets

opens

paints

pecks

peels

picks nose

pierces

piloting

pinches

pirouettes

places

plays

points

pounds with fist

praying

puckers cheeks

pulls

pulsates

pushes

punching

pouring

rains

raises

regenerates

removes

repairs

rescues

rides

rolling

rubbing

rubs

running

runs

sails

salts

saws

scratches

screams

shake

shaves

shits

shivers

shoots

shuffles (cards)

shuffles

sings

sips

sits

sitting on toilet

skipping

sleeping

smoking

smelling

smiling

sneezes

sparkles

spiking

spits

squeezes

staggers

stepping on

stops

strangles

stretching

strums

stuffs

sucks

sweeps

swims

swing

takes

talks

throws

tackles

tickles

ties

touches

turn

turns

urinates

uses

walk

washing

wave

whistles

whines

whips

wink

wishes

won't

wraps

wrestles

writing

yawning

yodelling

8. Number Shapes

Number shapes are images that look like number digits. As an example; Number digit "0" looks like an "Egg", a "Ball" or a "Hula Hoop". It can be any object you like as long as it's a lookalike object.

We use number shapes as "pegs", which are the objects that we use as storage - an alternative to using a memory palace, and as part of a Number To Image Generating System.

You can in fact use a memory palace with pegs which would make the Paired-Links much easier to memorize for long term.

To memorize a quick list of items, number shapes are the perfect and probably faster way of memorizing almost any short list you like, and remember it for the rest of the day with ease.

The idea of using Number Shapes is to memorize information by pair-linking it together.

Here are the Number Shapes from 0-10 which would allow you to memorize a list of 11 items.

Or more than 11 items if a story method is used as explained in Chain-Linking.

0 Egg	6 Golf-Club
1 Wand	7 Boomerang
2 Swan	8 Snowman
3 Butterfly	9 Balloon
4 Chair	10 Stick & Drum
5 Unicycle	

Here are the images for Number Shapes from 0-10

Here is an example of how you'd use the basic number shapes to memorize a quick list.

Remember we had a "To-Do List"? Let's use the same list but this time using the Number Shapes as the storage for the list.

We have;

9am: Buy Fuel for the car
9.30am: Call Dad
10am: Library
10.30am: Pay the bill
11am: Swim
12pm: Pick up groceries
1pm: Car Wash

Let's start with the digit "0" as the first number shape item which is an Egg.

Now let's Pair-Link "The Egg with Fuelling The car"

Imagine yourself with some eggs in your hand, and you are fuelling the car with those eggs!

You have now Paired the Link with The Egg and Fuel together. As you can see here there is not a need for a memory palace because we are simply using number shape items as a storage for what we wanted to memorize.

You can of course also use a memory palace to place your Paired-Links into the Trigger Locations which would make it much more memorable.

However, the idea of using pegs such as Number Shapes is so that you can quickly memorize a list without needing a memory palace.

Now let's connect the next item in the list which is to "Call

Dad".

The next number shape we'll use is digit "1" which is the "Magic Wand" object.

Imagine that you have a "Magic Wand" in your hand this time. You wave it and tap it in the air and your Dad appears in front of you, and at the same time you hear the sound of your phone ringing.

Next is the Swan, the number shape for "2". The item we need to memorize next is the Library.

Imagine a Huge Swan running around the Library and pecking into all the shelves and the books!

Got the idea? Great!

I'll let you practice with the rest of the items using the rest of the number shapes.

9. Number Rhymes

Number Rhymes are images that rhyme with or sound like number digits which are also used as pegs, which means they are also a storage mnemonic tool to memorize a list of items.

The use of Number Rhymes works the same way as the number shapes when we want to memorize a quick list of items.

It's also a very popular method used by a lot of public speakers, actors and stage performers alike.

Here are the basic 0-30 Number Rhymes that you can use to memorize a quick list for your needs

0 Hero	11 Elephant	22 Twitter
1 Bun	12 Elves	23 Trophy
2 Shoe	13 Typing	24 Tofu
3 Tree	14 Fountain	25 Trifle
4 Door	15 Fighting	26 Twix
5 Hive	16 Sardines	27 Tweezers
6 Sticks	17 Surfing	28 Terminate
7 Heaven	18 A Tin	29 Tasty Wine
8 Gate	19 Noting	30 Thirsty
9 Wine	20 Twin	
10 Hen	21 Chihuahua	

10. Story Method

We humans love stories. One of the simple reasons why we love stories is because our brain is naturally programmed to remember stories.

Our brain has the ability to see animated images that form the story. Just like a movie.

This method is also used for memorizing words, quotes, and text-books.

A story can be a short story like a "**Mini-Story**", or as long as you can make it - like a "**Long-Story**".

A mini story is created by a "**Paired-Link**", and longer stories are created by "**Chained-Links**".

Here is a quick example of a Paired-Link for A Mini-Story.

Let's say we have to memorize the following;
Egg | Shoes | Car | Book

Let's Pair-Link the Egg & Shoes for the mini story.

Imagine "you are cracking a huge Egg on your Shoes."
There you have it. You have just created a Mini-Story by Pair-Linking the first two items.

Now let's create a longer story by Chain-Linking the rest of the items or words.

Next is the Car. So we will link "Shoes" which was the previous item, with the next item "Car".

Imagine "you are taking off your Shoes, and start hitting your Car with it".

Next in the chain is the "Book". So we'll now link the previous item which is the "Car", with the next item which is the "Book".

Imagine "you are pulling a huge Book out of your Car".

And there you have it. Pair and Chain Linking is how you create a story with the information you have in your hand. With this method you can literally memorize almost anything you like!

Give it A Start Location OR A Memory Palace

Single Location Start: The example story above starts with you cracking an egg on your shoes. However, you still have to give this story a location to start with so you know where this happens. As it is "you" in this story, you have to exist somewhere. Where are you? Are you in the kitchen, garden, in a park, museum? Where are you? What is the starting location for your story?

You can create your story from a single location, and simply extend that location by adding your chain-links into your story.

Memory Palace: The other method would be to use a Memory Palace. Simply place Paired-Links or Chain-Links into each location in your memory palace

11. Visualizing & Imagination

We know that our brain sees animated images just like a movie before it can record or store the information we want to memorize, therefore improving visualisation is probably one of the most important aspects of having a trained brain.

The good news is that **Visualization is a skill you can learn!** It's just like learning any other skill. The more you do it the better you'll get at it. Just like riding a bicycle, you fall, fall, and then balance, and pedal away.

It's a skill that can be learned with the knowledge available, and the practice you put into it.

You get better and better with it as you practice more and more at it. I had one of the worst memories ever when I first started my journey in the art of memorizing.

With the knowledge and practice, you will develop to be at least 500% or more better than ever before.

As for myself I am 1000% better as I have now been practicing for many years and it has become a second nature to me.

It will be with you as well as long as you put some practice into it.

FOCUS: Deciding to remember.

Basic understanding of "How to remember and recall what you have memorized" is first to "Decide To Memorize It".

First, you need to decide that you want to remember, and that you have a desire to memorize that piece of information. This will activate and force your brain to think, focus more and take action.

But if you don't decide to remember it in the first place, then you will simply forget it because the brain did not care enough to remember it and therefore it sees it as a low value information.

So make a decision to decide to remember what you are going to memorize, be it a birthday, a daily to do list, work related, educational, personal, a speech, or whatever it may be.

To remember it, you have to memorize it.

To be able to recall what you memorize will **first** require you to really **understand how it works** and then **practice** until it becomes a second nature, and yes it does become a second nature, as all memory enthusiasts and experts will tell you. You'll be developing a better and stronger brain that will have the ability to memorize and recall anything you want.

Exercising your brain is like exercising your body, what happens if you lift weights 50 times a day for a month?

You will notice that your muscles are getting bigger and

stronger, and this is the same with your brain.

By applying memory techniques, you'll notice that your brain will get better, faster, stronger and better at problem solving.

How To Improve Visualization:

Ask each time you associate an image to an item or a piece of information, be it an object, a name, words, number etc.

* What does it look like?
* What does it sound like?
* What does it remind me of?

There are 5 Main elements to visualizing & imagination.
1. Using Our 5 Senses
2. Associations To Generate Images
3. Using Exaggerated Actions
4. Using Exaggerated Emotions
5. Remember To Practice

1. Using Our 5 Senses
Let's start activating your imagination.

1. Observation: Eyes

Our eyes are the physical tools to see everything. But we actually also see everything with our mind's eyes.

Follow this exercise: Look at what's in front of you. Wave your hands over what's in front of you. Notice at least 3 everyday items that are in front of you.

Now close your eyes, and try to see with your mind's eye what you just did. Did you recall what you just did?

Were you able to see what you did with your eyes closed?

Great. You have a wonderful memory! A memory that can be trained to memorize anything you like.

Colour: Now do the same action again, but this time, have a look at the colours of what's in front of you. Maybe there are some items there that are red, blue, yellow, or some of them are a mixture of colours? Notice what they are.

Shape: Next, have a look at the shapes of those items in front of you. Notice their outline shape, texture and how they look.

Size: Next, notice the size of those items in front of you, how big are they? How would you describe it?

2. Sound: Ears
Do any of the items in front of you make any specific sounds?

Do you have to cause an action to hear the sound of an item in front of you? What does it sound like?

3 . Aromas: Smell

How do those items smell? Can you recognise the smell of any of those items. What do they smell like?

4. Feel The Texture: Touch
Touch the items. What does the material feel like? Soft, hard, metal, plastic, leather, wood?

Feel the weight: If you were to lift it, how heavy would it be? What's its weight?

5. Flavors: Taste
Are any of these items edible? If you were to take a bite into each item, what would they taste like?

Can you associate it with a type of food, drink or tastes?

2. Associations To Generate Images

Whenever you have the need to memorize a piece of information, you must find an image for it.

Simply put; "A Tangible Item" that you can use to pair-link with either your pegs, or your memory palace.

Remember the list for the Peg method? Those pegs-images are ready made images that you should memorize before hand, so that you can memorize other information by pair-linking the two together. Associating Numbers, Words, Pictures Names, Cards, and Everything Else In Between.

Numbers: To memorize **numbers** we associate the number digits with images.

For example 00: Eggs | 01: Shield & Spear

We use a number system to memorize numbers such as The Shaper System, The Major, Or The Dominic System.

Words: To memorize **words** we associate each word with related images. For example;

Bulgaria: Bull
France: Eiffel-Tower
Iceland: Ice-Cubes

We use a word system to memorize words with or without a memory palace. We simply Pair-Link two words together, or Chain-Link them all.
Pictures: To memorize **pictures** we pair-link each image with a known peg image. We use an image system to memorize images.
When you want to memorize 10 different pictures, and you want to memorize those pictures in the correct order;

Simply add the number shapes from 1-10 into each picture by

Pair-Linking with an action. Mentally walk back and you'll remember them all.

Names & Faces: To memorize **names** we associate the names with images. We use a names system to memorize names.

When you have a Face & name to memorize; Think of an image that sounds like the name, and mentally attach that image to the face.

If and when you can't find one, use the Shaper System Alphabet Pegs with a mixture of Vowels & Consonants" and attach them to the face to remind you of the name.

Cards: To memorize **cards** we associate all cards into images . We use a card system to memorize cards.

Most people who like to memorize cards use a Person Or Objects Image for each card in the deck. This is what's known as a "1 Card System" which is a single image for a single card.

A 1 Card System simply places each card-image into a memory palace, mentally.

A 1 card system can be a "PA: Person Action" which is a method to memorize 2 cards at a time.

A 1 Card System is also used as "PAO: Person Action Object" which is a method to memorize 3 cards at a time.

A Two Card System would mean that you would assign a combination of two cards into a single image.

This is known as "2 Card-System". And we associate **everything else in between** into images. Each time you want to memorize some new information;

- You first must convert the new information into a list.
- Find a tangible image for each new item on the list.
- Use the correct system to memorize your list.

Associating Images With Number Digits

The Shaper System

To give you an idea of how we generate images by way of associations from the list above, here I provide you the methods of associating with images for the rest of the list.

To memorize Number Digits we use a method of association to generate images known as the "Number To Image Generator".

It's a good idea to have number digits as a pair from 00-99. This means that you can memorize two digits at a time by generating images that you can use as your pre-memorized pegs.

For example;

Using **The Shaper System**;
00 = Eggs
01 = Shield & Spear
02 = Dinosaur
03 = Fork
04 = Knife
and this list goes on until
99 = Balloons.

The images from the Shaper-System gives us 100 pegs. We can use these items as pegs storage to pair-link information.

Or we simply use them as items that represent all 100 to digit combinations to memorize numbers however long we like using a memory palace!

The Shaper-System is a ready-made system in a box. Meaning; the images, actions, objects, and everything else are all ready to be used out of the box.

You don't need to prepare any images for any of the shapes and pictures for any of the disciplines you would use to memorize information.

It's all ready to be learned, and ready to use.

Another good thing with the shaper system is that you will have the ability to edit any of the materials you like to convert it into your own system!

"The Dominic System", and "The Major System".
There are two other Number To Image Generators known as "The Dominic System", and "The Major System".

The Dominic System is a "Number To Person-Image Generating System" with the number digits from 00-99. The Dominic System uses the numbers from 0-9 as the base and assigns a letter to each number as follows;

$0 - O \mid 1 - A \mid 2 - B \mid 3 - C \mid 4 - D \mid 5 - E \mid 6 - S \mid 7 - G \mid 8 - H \mid 9 - N$

So the first two digits would be;
00: OO

Next and so on until 99;
01: OA | 02: OB | 03: OC | 04: OD | ... 99: NN

This also provides 100 images. Since The Dominic System is a Number To Person Image Generator, we use each digit with the matching initials and find Persons with A Name & Surname.

As an example;

00: OO – Olive Oyl
01: OA – Orlando Anderson
02: OB – OBama
...
99: NN – NiNa

Once you have 100 Persons, you then think of their Actions, and then their prop, such as clothing or an item that person carries or uses most of the time.

You then pair link the digits as PA: Person Action.

Here is an example;
00: Olive Oyl is Cooking Spinach.
02: OBama is Giving A Speech.
If you happen to get these four digits to memorize, this is how it would look;
PA: 00 02
Olive Oyl is Giving A Speech.

Or if it was the other way round;
PA: 02 00: OBama is Cooking Spinach.

The Major System is a "Number To Image Generating System" with the number digits from 00-99. The Major System uses the numbers from 0-9 as the base and assigns a Consonant-Letter to each number as follows;

$0 - s,z \mid 1 - t,d \mid 2 - n \mid 3 - m \mid 4 - r \mid 5 - 1 \mid 6 - sh, ch, jh \mid 7 - k \mid 8 - f \mid 9 - b, p$

So the first two digits would be;
00: ss
Next and so on until 99;
01: st
02: sn

...

99: pp

This also provides 100 images. Since The Major System is a Number To Image Generator, we use each digit with the matching consonant sounds to make a word, and then convert that word into an image

As an example;
00: ss – Sauce
01: st – Suit
02: sn – Sun
03: sm: Sumo

...

99: pp: Pipe

Once you have 100 images, you then think of their Actions. You then pair link the digits as OAO: Object Action Object

Here is an example;
00: Sauce (Ketchup)
02: Sun

If you happen to get these four digits to memorize, this is how it would look, you would imagine something like

OAO: 00 02
Ketchup Sauce Poured Over The Sun

Or you would add a person into the scene such as yourself or another person - you would use POAO; Person Object Action (Linked with) Object.

And you would imagine something like
PO AO: 00 02
You/Him/Her Holding A Bottle Of Ketchup Sauce, Pouring It All Over The Sun.

Or if it was the other way round, you would imagine something like;

OAO: 00 02
Sun is Burning The Ketchup Sauce

PO AO: 00 02
You/Him/Her Holding The Sun and Burning A Bottle Of Ketchup Sauce with it.

You can create a list of the persons yourself, <u>or check out this website **"PeopleByInitials.com"** for ideas to create your 100 persons.</u>

3. Using Exaggerated Actions

As you know already, we pair-link two images together by an action. And we create a mini-story by pair-linking or chain-linking by those actions.

They will be memorable by all means. However, using exaggerated actions will strengthen the story and therefore make it even more memorable.

As an example;

Let's use "Superman" as an example person for the number digits "00", His Action as "Flying Into The Object

So we have PA: 00: "Superman is Flying"

Let's now use another person with another action

PA: 01: "Batman is Punching".

Now if we get; 00 01 , This translates to PA as;
PA: Superman is Punching

Or the other way round; 01 00
PA: Batman is Flying.

Now let's use exaggerated actions here to make it more memorable!

00 01: Superman is Punching while farting! Oh what a terrible odor coming from him! You can hear it with every punch! He is embarrassed!

Or the other way round; 01 00;
01 00: Batman is Flying while Laughing Out Loud. He may have just realised he could fly, but soon drops to the floor all confused!

Adding exaggerated actions to your paired linked mini-stories will certainly make the story much more memorable indeed.

4. Using Exaggerated Emotions

As with using exaggerated actions, we also use emotions to make our stories more memorable.

We are made of our emotions, and it's one of the main reasons why we are by default able to remember more than we think. We use our emotions to make decisions with everything we do through the day. And by the end of the day our brain can remember most of the day's activities.

We are emotional beings. We can be very Sad, Angry, Stressed or Violent. But at the same time we can be a loving person, full of joy, enthusiasm, laughter, and ambition. Adding emotions to your stories will double the strength of the paired-link mini-story and therefore become much more memorable.

As an example;

Let's go back to Superman and Batman but this time notice their emotions.

00 01: Superman is Punching while farting! Oh what a terrible odor coming from him! You can hear it with every punch! He is **embarrassed**!

Or the other way round; 01 00;
01 00: Batman is Flying while Laughing Out Loud. He may have just realised he could fly, but soon drops to the floor all **confused**

Adding exaggerated actions to your paired linked mini-stories will certainly make the story much more memorable indeed.

In fact you may sometimes have difficulty forgetting it for a good while, unless otherwise you practice spaced repetition which is the last subject I will cover.

5. Remember To Practice

Visualization is a skill you can learn by simply practicing it over and over.

Using your 5 senses to learn every image you generate, along with adding exaggerated actions & emotions will double and triple your imagination.

12. Spaced Repetition

Spaced repetition is where you would have to review your system's images, pegs lists, memory palaces, and the subjects you have memorized over a period of timed intervals.

Review your system's images for Numbers, Words, Pictures Names, Cards, and Everything Else

Review your Peg-Storage images using the lists from your peg method.

Review your memory palaces each, room by room, and all the items in each location.

Review the subjects you have memorized such as The Presidents, History Facts, Dates, Speeches and everything else you want to keep in your long term memory.

Mentally review all of the above at timed intervals.

Timed Interval Reviews For Long Term Memory

After you have memorized your subject's list, you will have to mentally review your steps again a few times over a period of time if you want to keep it memorized long term or permanently.

The recommended time interval for reviewing your subjects again is as follows;

- Review after 10 minutes
- Review after 1 hour
- Review after 8 hours
- Review in 24 hours
- Review 1 week later
- Review 1 month later
- Review again in 3 months
- Review again in 6 month
- Review again in 12 months.

If you follow the timed intervals to review all the long term memory materials, you'll have them programmed into your mind forever!

And you will have the ability to memorize almost anything you like, at any time you like.

Spaced Repetition Tools You Can Use To Review Your Materials.

* Your **PC** or Laptop is your best friend for your reviews! Most of the images and notes can be saved on your PC or Laptop's hard-drive.

* **Spreadsheets** are very helpful to review your materials.
* **Anki** helps you setup your images in a flash-card format.

 Mnemosyne is another platform you can use to save your materials for reviews.

* **Art Of Memory Software** (Recommended) is a brilliant software for saving and reviewing.

Learning is the key to applying the methods successfully. Practice is the key to memorizing successfully

Part 4
The Shaper System

- The Shaper System : General Background.
- The Number Shapes Of The Shaper System.
- The English Alphabet Shapes From A-Z.
- How It All Started.
- Three Main Benefits Of The Shaper System.
- 5 Ways To Use The Shaper System Images.

Part 4
The Shaper System

Visit paolist.com to download The Full Shaper System and all of the materials to enjoy practicing your memory skills.

<u>DOWNLOAD BOTH VERSIONS – FREE! on paolist.com</u>

The Shaper System : General Background

The Shaper System was developed by **<u>Erol Ozvatan</u>** with the initial intention of converting 2 digit numbers and letters of the Alphabet from their outline shapes into visual lookalike images.

As an example; The image for "19" is an Elephant in the shaper system. This is because the digits can be easily visualized as a side view of an Elephant with its "Back Tail", "Big Ear" and "Trunk".

Another example is "20" which is "Snail". We see the outline shapes of the digits which reflect the impression of a "Snail" with the digit '2' as the front of the body and digit '0' as the shell.

The Shaper System is used to memorize; Number Digits | Binary Digits | Playing cards | Images | Words | Memory Palaces | Lists | Names & Faces.

Numbers And Images Of The Shaper System
The basic Number Shape System generates images from 0-9. The Shaper System was further developed to generate images from 00-99.

The shaper system is a 2 digit "Number To Image Generator" that generates an instant 2 digit lookalike image from 00-99, totalling 100 images. With the addition of the basic Number Shapes, a total of 110 images can be used.

The Number Shapes Of The Shaper System.

Numbers Shapes 0-9

0 - Egg
1 - Magic Wand | Lighter
2 - Duck | Coat Hanger | Pigeon
3 - Butterfly | Lips
4 - Chair | Knife
5 - Unicycle
6 - Golf-Club
7 - Boomerang
8 - Snowman
9 - Balloon

Numbers Shapes 00-09
00 = Eggs
01 = Shield & Spear
02 = Dinosaur
03 = Fork
04 = Chopping board & Knife | Knife
05 = Hand
06 = Frying Pan
07 = Paint Roller
08 = Pool Ball - Black Ball with 8 on it.
09 = Boxer's Glove | Hook Punch

Numbers Shapes 10-19
10 = a Stick & Drum | Fatman
11 = two Drum Sticks
12 = Playground Slide | Needle & Thread |
13 = Arrow & Bow | Pregnant woman
14 = Toilette | Heart - Valentine's Day | Red Rose |
Necklace
15 = Man pushing a Disabled Chair | or just a Disabled

Chair
16 = a Hand Pointing Finger
17 = Harp | Woodpecker
18 = Broom & Snowman
19 = Elephant

Numbers Shapes 20-29
20 = Snail
21 = Dollar sign
22 = Pair of High Heels Shoes
23 = Swan - Neck-body-tail
24 = Alarm Clock (Associated)
25 = Christmas Tree | Santa's sleigh (Associated)
26 = Kettle
27 = Trowel
28 = Crocodile
29 = Gondola and man

Numbers Shapes 30-39
30 = Heart | Lips
31 = Lips smoking cigarette
32 = Teeth | Shark |
33 = Seagull
34 = Goat |Goat Milk
35 = Crane Hook
36 = Lips smoking pipe
37 = Rocket
38 = Beetle Car
39 = Lollipop | Lips Licking Lollipop

Numbers Shapes 40-49
40 = Concrete Mixer Truck | Spade
41 = Jet Ski | Man Jet Skiing
42 = Horse Head and Neck curve
43 = Fish
44 = Umbrella (the second 4 flipped horizontally)

45 = Snake
46 = Seahorse
47 = Chihuahua
48 = Pick up Van (8 tilted down as the wheels)
49 = Mice

Numbers Shapes 50-59
50 = Tractor | Tractor Wheel
51 = Pipe Wrench
52 = Playing Cards (Associated)
53 = Hand & Cuffs | Cuffs
54 = Chair | Handy-Chair
55 = Wheelbarrow | 2 Hands High Five (Associated)
56 = Forklift
57 = Blacksmith Anvil | Hammer
58 = Scooter (8 tilted down as wheels)
59 = Bull

Numbers Shapes 60-69
60 = Monkeys Tail and Body | Eats "Banana"
61 = Fishing Tackle
62 = Cat (6 is head and Ear, 2 is Body & tail)
63 = Bee
64 = Golf Club & Golf Flag
65 = Muscle Arm & Bicep
66 = Two Cherries with a leaf
67 = Rope Hanging from its Wood-Hanger
68 = Pram
69 = Yin Yang

Numbers Shapes 70-79
70 = Straw in a cocktail glass
71 = Fire Extinguisher
72 = Water pump

73 = Camel
74 = Semi Automatic Handgun
75 = Exercise Bike
76 = Saxophone
77 = Two Handle Electric Drill | Two man Rowing | Two bent legs
78 = Shopping cart (8 tilted down as wheels)
79 = Axe and Farmer | Axe

Numbers Shapes 80-89
80 = Baby Dummy
81 = Violin and bow | Guitar
82 = Woman & Long Hair | Hair
83 = Mask (Tilt to the right)
84 = Bride and Groom (arm) - Flowers & Bride holding arm with the broom and walking.
85 = Girl on a Unicycle | Unicycle
86 = Girl blowing a Whistle
87 = Frog Eyes & Mouth
88 = Weights
89 = Snorkel

Numbers Shapes 90-99
90 = Ninja Turtle | Turtle
91 = Space suit | Spaceman
92 = Lion
93 = Butterfly
94 = Dolphin
95 = Squirrel
96 = Key & Padlock
97 = Old Man & his walking stick
98 = Biker with helmet | Bicycle
99 = Balloon

The English Alphabet Shapes From A-Z

A = Peg | Eiffel Tower | Tent
B = Sunglasses
C = Banana
D = Bow | Tongue | Protractor
E = Comb | Trident
F = Toothbrush | Crutch
G = Pacman | Ear | G-Clamp
H = Step Ladder
I = Flute | Needle | Stick | Candle
J = Shinty | Shofar | Alphorn | Hockey
K – Table [tilted] | Whizzy Ride – Bike | Ballerina Dancing
L – A Gun with a silencer | Ruler | Allen Key
M – Spider
N – Compass [North] | Fence | Mach-Sticks
O – Bracelet | Tyre | Ring | Ball | Hula Hoop
P – Flag on a pole | Sword [tilted]
Q – Magnifier | Tiara | Bicycle Pedal
R – Pincer | Pliers | Badge
S – Snake | Hook
T – Cross | Hammer | T-Ruler
U – Cup | Horse Shoe | Magnet
V – Necklace | Ice-Cream Cone
W – Vampire Teeth
X – Scissors | Plasters
Y – Slingshot | Funnel | Wine Glass
Z – Zebra | Escalator | Spring

How It All Started

When I used persons with the Dominic system, most of my persons didn't have any objects or any actions I could apply. And it was somewhat confusing to me when I did, and thus took me a long time to memorize.

So I tried to mix and match with the major system. The major system is consonant-letter to digits. Again it was taking me longer than I wanted to translate the digits and apply the actions.

However, with the number shapes I could see the images much more easily and much faster. I also didn't have to translate it from Dominic's letters into persons, or translate it from the major into words, and then create images and apply the actions. The process seemed to be a lot of work.

With the number shapes, it was easy, no translation needed. They are just shapes that look like the digits, or the digits that look like the shapes.

The images I have for the shapes also have their own natural actions, or can be created very easily with paired-linking.

So each shape-image performs the action to the next, or leaves a clue which reminds me of the first 2 digits. So it's a kind of system in a box. The Shaper-System-Spreadsheet is available to download. Ready to use.

To start practising the method, say the Image and its action Out Loud as soon as you see the two digit number, and visualise the image and the action at the same time as you practice.

So when you see 00 for example, you'd say "Eggs, Breaking, Yolk running" out loud - and see the eggs in your mind.

01 = You say "Spear Stabbing through"

02 = You say "Dinosaur, Blowing Burning Fire "
03 = You say "Fork, Sticking into"
04 = You say "Knife, Cutting"
etc, etc.

Then apply the paired-link action.

00 01 – You'd say "Runny Yolk on Spear" (Breaking the Spear)
04 00 – "Cutting the Egg"
02 03 – Burning Fork
01 02 – Spear Through Dinosaur

After practising it for a few days, it will just jump out at you as an image without the need to say it out loud.

A lot of the images have their own clue when the action is applied, meaning you won't necessarily have to see the action or the object, because the clue on the object provides the first 2 digits.

For example "30" Is Kissing, and the clue is "Red-Heart" image stuck/stamped on the next object. "00" is Eggs, All I see is Runny Yolk on the next object as a clue for the "00".

It doesn't need the action because of the clue.

It is also used with existing systems such as the Dominic or Major System, or any other independent system.

00 – Superman
04 – Cutting (with a Knife)
02 – Dinosaur
Superman Cutting a Dinosaur (with a Knife)

00 – Superman
02 – Dinosaur (Blowing Burning Fire)
04 – Knife

Superman Blowing Fire On a Knife

You would of course also add "Emotions" to it wherever you can to make it more memorable.

So superman burning his hands on fire, after blowing it on the knife - which is not a great feeling.

The above sample is PAO, but you could simply use PA if you are using the Dominic PA system. "Superman Blowing Fire".

Three Main Benefits Of The Shaper System;

1. It does not rely on the Major Phonetics spelling.
So you don't have to use any consonants, and then find a word, and then find an image etc. Because it's a self working system with its objects and its actions.

It's a system in a box that can be learned in a very short time.

2. It can be learned in almost any language!
The great thing about images is they are the same in every language!

For example 19 is an Elephant.
The shape of the Elephant looks the same in all languages. It's a number to image generator, and the image is the same all round the world.

3. It can be used with any existing person or object based system variation, as explained above.

5 Ways To Use The Shaper System Images

The shaper system has all the images premade from 00-99. This allows the memorizer to use them in 5 different ways.

1. Number System: Use it for your Number System to memorize any number digits to any length.

2. Pegs-As-Storage: Use all 100 images as pegs to store data. No need for a memory palace.

3. Mark The Path: Use a shape for each 5th location in a memory palace to remember the order and the position of the path.

4. Mini-Palaces: Use each shape as a "5 Stop Mini-Palace" with **Left | Top | Right | Bottom | Middle**

5. Expandable Memory Palaces: Use each image to expand the shaper palace to 500 locations.

You can do this simply by mentally adding each image into each corresponding Background image, and you'll have a 5 stop Mini-Palace within each room, expanding the palace to 500 locations..

Part 5

Memory Applications

Part 5
Memory Applications

Now that you have a better idea of how our memory & memorizing works, let's dive into how we use these in real life applications.

Where Are My Keys?

One of the problems we face almost every day is that we keep forgetting where we leave our everyday items we use throughout the day such as our keys, wallet, purse, glasses. Fortunately there is an easy solution to this.

All you have to do is to use the same simple method of memorizing when you have the need to remember where you left your things.

Here is how you do it;

What you do is that you imagine your "item" next to the "location" you choose "at the place you are in."

So let's say you are at a friend's house. Choose a place where you will leave your keys. Place your keys at your chosen spot, and while doing so imagine a "Dog's Head Barking" at your spot. So if that spot was next to the "Kettle", then you imagine a Dog's Head Barking next to the "Kettle". Now add and action to it. Imagine the Dog is actually "Eating" your keys!

You can apply the same method with other item such as putting your glasses down at a spot you want to remember. It works the same way as the Dog example. But this time you can use a "Cat". So you can remember more of your items and remember the exact spot of your items. Just use different animals for different items. You can also use persons if you want to take it further.

Memorizing anything works the same way no matter what you memorize. We connect a link between what we want to remember with what we already know. So it's the same method when we memorize where we leave our everyday items.

Another one is to memorize where you leave you car. I never used to be able to remember where I left my car in the car park, at what level and the number position of the car. With this easy method it's a piece of cake.

What you do is to use 0-9 Number Shapes. So if you parked your car at Level 9, at the 18th position, then you would imagine "A Balloon On A String" stuck to the left side of your car, and the "Snowman With Broom" on the right side of the car, which represents "18" which gives you the number position of your car.

So by just using your imagination, you played the movie of your car with a balloon, and a snowman with a broom, and memorized exactly where your car will be at the car park.

How To Memorize Phone Numbers

To memorize strings of numbers you first need to have a number system with 100 images from 00-99 - such as the Shaper System, with a number shape added as the action.

You then Attach that to the Name or the Organization.

Memorize A Phone Number Of A Person

5 Digits Method.

If you are using Persons in your 2 digit system, this is how it would look;

Say you want to memorize the phone number of a friend called "Alex". Let's say the digits were;01234 56789

Let's use the shaper system as an example;
01 = Superman
2 = Blowing Fire (Action)
34 = Milk

First, you'd imagine Alex standing in front of you.

On his Left hand side you'd see;
Superman- Blowing Fire – Into A Glass Of Milk "that Alex is holding in his left hand."

Now the next 5 digits;
56 = Batman
7 – Hammering
89 = Snorkel

On his Right hand side you'd see;
Batman is Hammering the Snorkel that Alex is holding in his right hand"

3 Digits Method.

You can also do this with 3 digits at a time.

Eliminate the Zero 0, because most phone numbers start with 0.

Now we have; 123 | 456 | 789

Again, use your 2 digit person with a number shape from 0-9 as an action.

Use the person's left, top, and right side as the locations.

12 – Abbie
3 = Kissing

Left side of Alex. (12 3)

Abbie is Kissing Alex on his left cheek.

45 – Spiderman
6 – Frying Pan

To the head of Alex (45 6)

Spiderman is Hitting Alex over the Head with a Frying pan.

78 – Matrix
9 – Boxing

On the Right side of Alex (78 9)

Matrix is Boxing/Punching Alex on his right cheek/chin.

Memorize A Phone Number Of An Organizations

If you want to memorize the phone number of a shop or organization, you can simply use the same method.

Let's say it was the Barber shop

Simply add 5 digits at a time inside the barber shop to two spots of your choice.

And do the same for all other organizations.

A Quick and Easy Method to Memorize numbers fast!

You can use this simple method on the fly, in any situation to memorize a phone number of a person or organization very quickly by using your existing persons.

It works by memorizing;

The first Person (2 digits) + The Surname Of The Second Person. (2 digits)

+ a Number Shape Action (1 digit)

+ The first Person (2 digits) + The Surname Of The Second Person. (2 digits)

Once you have that, you repeat the new name & the action by rote memory a few times. And you'll be able to recite it back to the person immediately, or at a later time by simply decoding it back to the digits.

Here is an example showing how to memorize a phone number using this method;

Let's use the earlier example phone number - 1234 5 6789

I have eliminated the first digit which is "0" because most phone numbers start with that so I don't have to memorize it.

I already know it starts with zero.

So we have the following digits with the matching names.;
12: Abbie Smith
34: Celine Dion

5: Unicycle
67: Sergen Yalçın
89: Hande Yener

This translates to;
12 34 = Abbie Dion (First Name + Second Person's Surname)

5 = Unicycle – Riding & Kicking

67 89 = Sergen Yener (First Name + Second Person's Surname)

So now the first Name & Surname that covers the first 4 digits reads simply as follows;

"Abbie Dion" = 12 34

Now add the number shape with its action to the first person;

Riding a Unicycle & Kicking = 5

Lastly add the next 4 digits using the person and the second person's surname.

67 89 = Sergen Yener

The whole sentence here would be;
"Abbie Dion is Riding a Unicycle and Kicks Sergen Yener."

There you have it. By having 100 persons in your memory system, you can memorize phone numbers fast using this simple method.

I do use the 5 digits method myself rather than 4 or 6 digits because most phone numbers are 10 digits, so I find it much easier to create the images and attach it to the person with his/her phone number.

The Re-Action Method

If I have a single digit left to use, I simply use a number shape as a "Re-Action"and link it to the first person or the situation.

Let's make up a 10 digit phone number; Bold digits are number shapes and their actions. You'll notice I've added a zero "0" as the Reaction back to the first person as follows;

Phone Number: 1234 **5** 6789 **0**

Here is how it would look;
12 - Abbie Smith
43 - Celine Dion
5 - Unicycle - Riding & Kicking

1243 5 = Abbie Dion Unicycle "Riding & Kicking" Sergen Yener, and

6789 0 = Sergen Yener Cracks a huge Egg on the head of Abbie Dion

This will then give you 10 digits with a number shape added as the "Re-Action".

The "PAP" Method with 2 Digit Action

Another method is to use a 2 digit Action to make it up to 10 digits.

It's just as simple as adding a 2 digit action rather than a 1 digit action.

1234 = Abbie Dion
56 = Forklifting
7890 = Super Alco (First Name + Second Person's Surname))

Now your sentence would look like this;

"Abbie Dion Fork-Lifting Super Alco".

Which gives you 1234 **56** 7890

Person + Second Person Surname | 2 Digit Action | Person + Second Person Surname.

You would of course have your number system as 100 persons, 100 actions and 100 Objects. The rest is to simply practice and apply it to your situations.

Digit To Letter Count Word Method;

This method works best for memorizing short digit numbers such as pin numbers, but phone numbers can also be memorized using the letter count method;

You basically assign a word to each number digit count.

So a "1" only has a single letter count of 1 such as "a, I"

2 needs a 2 letter word such as "at, on, no, me" etc

3 needs a 3 letter word such as "not, yes, why, may"

How it works is by assigning words to the number digits as the examples;

1 – a, I
2 – am, at, on, no, me, go
3 – not, yes, why, may, had, did, fun
4 – have, come, gone, look, done
5 – Break, Pizza
6 – haven't, hadn't, monday, yellow
7 – Sizzled, Cuddled
8 – drizzled, highjack, maximize
9 – Crunchier, Santander, Interested
0 – here you can simply use a number shape for the image and the action.

1 2 3 4 5 6 7 8 9
"I am not done, pizza cooked sizzled drizzled Crunchier!"

Now as you can see, even with the premade words it's still a little hard to memorize the phone number.

You can still use this method if you prepare well with premade words, or simply make up the words by finding some relevant words that are in harmony with the sentence.

However, I would recommend this for short numbers such as 4

digit pin numbers and or any other short numbers.

For a fast method of memorizing a phone number of a person I would recommend all the methods mentioned above the letter count method.

They work every time without a fail!

How To Memorize Words

How to memorize words to make any subject easier to learn

Learning how to memorize a list of words will help you to take on any subject and memorize it.

- Each time you have a list of words, associate and convert them into images.
- Each time you convert them into images, go through the questions below;
- Once you find the images for each word, you can either place each image into a premade Memory Palace, or assign it to a pre-memorized peg list.
- Or you can pair-link two words together, and again
- place it into the location or the peg to store the words.

The words system can be used for memorizing;

Books, poems, quotes, lines in plays, names, songs, facts, and everything else in between!

Convert the word into a tangible object

Let's say that the first word in your list was an "Egg".

You can simply imagine an Egg sitting in your fridge.

This would not require you to convert it into an image as it's already a tangible image you can visualize very easily.

Intangible Abstract images

So what happens when you don't have a ready-made image?

We will chunk the word down into bite size manageable words, and find a final image for it.

No matter what abstract word you get, you must always find an image for it. Remember that our brain memorizes words only through supporting images. So you must convert all abstract words into tangible images.

Let's see an example of a word list to memorize;

Words to memorize;

Trust | Address | Super | Punch | Extend | Jotter

Now let's go through questions to find the images for the list of these words;

What does it look like? What type of object is it?

What does it sound like? What Rhymes with it? What sound does it make?

What does it remind you of? Does it remind you of another object, person, place?

What color is it? Is it one color? Or a mixture of colors?

What size is it? How big would you say this object is?

By answering each question, you will be able to find images for each word.

What does Trust look like?

To me, it looks like "two people shaking hands on a trust agreement"

What does it sound like or rhymes like?

What kind of sound does it or could it make?

In my example, the sound of a firm handshake makes a 'clap'.

What does it remind you of?

Does it remind you of another object, person, place?

It reminds me of two businessmen shaking hands.

What colour is it? Is it one colour? Or a mixture of colours?

I see the arms of 2 businessmen, both wearing blue suits and white shirts

What size is it? How big would you say this object is?

Two Lifelike arms and hands.

So what happens when you can't find an easy image for it?
First we chunk the word into at least two or more parts. Then we find an image for each chunk.

By adding those chunked images, we arrive at a final image for the word.

Our next word is "Address".

Let's chunk it into two parts with the question of;

 "What does it sound like or Rhymes Like?

To me it sounds and rhymes like "Ad" + " Dress".

So I can now use a tangible image as "A Dress"

Let's now ask the rest of the questions;

What does a Dress look like? What type of Dress is it?

I now have to choose a type of dress. When I think of a dress, I immediately think of a "Wedding Dress".

What colour is it? Is it one colour or a mixture of colours?

This is an easy one. Most wedding dresses are white, so I'll go with a white dress.

What size is it? How big would you say this object is?

It's the size of a person who would fit in it, so it's lifelike size.

I'm sure you got the idea of finding images for the abstract words.

Now let's find the images for the rest of the words, and then we will place them into storage.

Super: I think of Superman.

Punch: I think of a "Boxer's Glove".

Extend: I chunk the word here into: Ex "Eggs" + tend "Tent" = **Eggs** In A Tent.

Jotter: I think of a "Jotter Pad".

Now let's see how we can memorize our words, with our images.

Use the Memory Palace Method - With Six Locations.

 Prepare a palace with as many locations needed for each word.

We have six words so we will need six locations to store six words.

Words-Images to memorize;

Trust: Handshake

Address: A Wedding Dress

Super: Superman

Punch: Boxer's Glove

Extend: Eggs In A Tent

Jotter : Jotter Pad

Simply place each image into each location in your memory palace. Mentally walk the journey to see each image. And translate it back to words while seeing the images in your mind.

Memory Palace With 3 Locations using the Pair-Link Method

Prepare 3 locations palace to memorize 2 words at a time by pair-linking both images.

Trust + Address = Handshake + A Wedding Dress

It's simple enough. Just imagine and visualize yourself; "Handshaking with a Wedding Dress"

And place that image into the first location in your memory palace.

You now have two words memorized in a single location.

Next two Pair-Link:

Super + Punch = Superman + Boxer's Glove

Imagine and Visualize; Superman Punching With A Boxer's Glove

Last Pair-Link

Extend + Jotter = Eggs In A Tent + Jotter pad

Imagine and Visualize; Eggs In A Tent with Jotter Pads coming out of each egg.

Memorizing Words As A Continuous Story

The Chain-Linking Method

Another way to memorize these six words is by creating a continuous story using the chain-linking method.

Words to memorize;

Trust | Address | Super | Punch | Extend | Jotter

Images:

Handshake | Wedding Dress | Boxer's Glove | Eggs In A Tent | Jotter Pad

Chain-Link example with The Story Method Using a Single Starter Location

You are at a wedding. You go to the bride, and handshake with her wedding dress instead of her hand. You notice she is getting married to Superman who is sitting next to her. He didn't like the idea of you handshaking her dress, so Superman punches you wearing a Boxer's Glove and carries you to his tent in which you are surprised to find is full of huge eggs. You pick up one of the eggs, crack it open, and inside you find a Jotter Pad.

Here we used a starting location that would make sense to the story.

However you can simply choose a memory palace with a single room as your starting location, and make your story happen in it.

I personally memorize 3 words at a time. It gives me a fast chain-link for the mini-story. I then place this into the first location in my memory palace, and use the next 3 by chain linking a mini story, and place that into my second location, and so on if I were to memorize a long list of words.

Memorize The Words With Pegs

Another way to memorize words is by using a peg list. And pair-link the words with your pegs.

Words to memorize;

Trust | Address | Super | Punch | Extend | Jotter

Images:

Handshake | Wedding Dress | Boxer's Glove | Eggs In A Tent | Jotter Pad

Pre-memorized Number Shape Pegs from 1-6

Magic Wand | Swan | Butterfly | Chair | Unicycle | Golf-Club

So let's Pair-Link **"Magic-Wand" with "Handshake"**

Imagine and Visualize; You are Handshaking with a Magic Wand.

Next is **Swan** with the **Wedding Dress**;

Imagine and Visualize; A Swan is Pecking Into The Wedding Dress.

Next is **Butterfly** with **Superman**

Imagine and Visualize; A Butterfly Flying with Superman's Cape.

Next is **Chair** with **Boxer's Glove**

Imagine and Visualize; A Chair is being punched by a Boxer's Glove.

Next is **Unicycle** with **Eggs In A Tent**

Imagine and Visualize; A Huge Unicycle running into a Eggs In A Tent.

Next is **Golf-Club** with **Jotter Pad**

Imagine and Visualize; You are swinging a Golf-Club into a pile of Jotter Pads.

Pair Linking, And Or Chain Linking Word Images To Your Pegs

Remember what we did when we pair-linked and chain-linked the items together?

Why not do the same with the pegs?

You'll have less pegs to use and more words to memorize.

- Pair link the two words first, and link it to the first peg.
- Or Chain Link a mini-story and link that to the first peg.
- And do the same with the rest of the word-images.

How did you do? Have you managed to memorize all six words?

Great! You're now on your way to having a winning word power memory in your hands for life.

Here are some more word examples to give you some more ideas;

Beauty – The Beast from the movie Beauty and the Beast. I remember it very well. The Beast character from the cartoon reminds me of the word Beauty and I can just imagine that image to remind me of it.

Bravery: Mel Gibson Fighting Very "Bravely" in the movie Brave heart. So Mel Gibson is the image for me for the word Bravery.

Courage – This is a little different, I imagine an old car which was my old Ford Escort that used to give me all sorts of trouble, it was an old banger.

Cour – Car | **age** – Old = Old Car (My old Escort).

So my Old Ford Escort is the tangible image I use.

Coldness – Eskimo person | Ice Cubes Nested | A Nurse who is cold and shivering.

Charity – Oxfam is the most famous Charity shop, and the logo of it is my image.

Also, Cha is Tea in many languages, so a Cha Tea could also be a good one to use.

Strength – Muscular Arm

Romance – Rome & Lovers Kissing. The famous Pisa Tower and a couple kissing.

Luck – Shamrock four leaf clover

Victory – V sign with fingers

Wealth – A pile of paper money bills (Stack of dollar bills or any type of money)

I see Bill Gates as soon as I see the word Wealth.

Service – Hotel reception Bell.

Customer Service – Headband | Hands free Headset with a Microphone.

Sleep – Pillow

Memory – Brain

Thought – Hands on my Head

Energy – Albert Einstein (E = Mc2) | Laser & Electric Cable

Pair Link Them Together

Once we find the matching images, we can then pair link the two together in a way that makes sense.

Examples;

Violence – Violins.
My nephew is a musician hitting me over the head with his Violin. I hit back with my violin. Some violence there.

Service – Hotel reception Bell.
Imagine you keep hitting the bell at a Hotel Reception and nobody comes and you keep shouting "Service please, anyone here?"

Coldness – Cold Nurse.
Your Nurse arrives at your house cold and shivering and puts on the heat/radiators etc.

Beauty – The Beast is Marrying the Beauty walking down the aisle.

Once you practice these images, initially with a mini-story-link a few times, it will just appear as tangible images and you won't even need the story-link anymore.

How To Memorize Foreign Words

Now that you have a good idea about how to memorize words, you can use the same skills to memorize foreign words!

We use the same methods to memorize foreign words. First we find images for both the English word and the foreign word. And then we pair link them together by an action and emotion, and place it in the relatively close place that would make sense.

For example; "Apple" in English is "Elma" in Turkish.

First, and as always, we have to find an image for both. Apple is already a nice image so we can use that as the peg that we already know.

Now we have to associate "Elma" with "Apple" so that we can link them together by an action and emotion, and place that image to a location that would remind you of where you'd find an Apple in the real world.

Make sure to ask the main three questions first to find the images for the foreign word.

What does it sound or rhymes like?

What does it look like?

What does it remind you of?

"Elma" sounds like "ill man". So I'll use that as my mnemonic support to act as the reminder trigger.

Let's now take a few seconds to imagine this Apple at your kitchen table in a bowl where you'd keep them.

Imagine "a man eating a huge Apple, but gets sick after eating it, and becomes an "ill man".

This scene will then remind you of the foreign word when you replay this scene in your mind a few times. And you'll have the ability to recall it at a later time when you need it.

How To Memorize The Lines In A Play

Your word skills are going to be very useful to you if and when you are faced with taking a role in a play on the stage. Or perhaps you are already a stage performer and want to improve your skills further.

Rote Memorize Your Lines

When you get your lines, simply go over your lines a few times by rote memory.

This is to simply repeat the lines over and over until you have them memorized.

Pick A Word From Your First Line. Use this as the Keyword reminder.

What you need is a mnemonic reminder image to give you the indication of what you have to say in your first line.

Let's say your first line is; **"I'll be waiting for you at the bar. See you soon."**

Next, choose a word that you can convert into an image immediately

So let's go over what you are looking for in a tangible image, so it's easier to remember. Don't go for abstract words unless you absolutely have to. Always find an easy tangible image for the word you choose. For example; If the word was an "Egg", then it will be easy to remember as it's already a physical, tangible object.

Let's say you choose the keyword "**The Bar**" from your first few lines which is easy to imagine as it's already a tangible image.

Imagine an image of a Bar at a typical airport.

Next, look for the "Cue Word" from The Other Actor, so that you can start your first line.

To do this; you look to hear your chosen word, or the last word, known as the "cue" word of the other actor. So when you hear the key word that you pick, you know that it is your turn to start your first line soon.

Let's say the line from the other actor was "Meet me at the airport." before you start your first line.

Pick a word from this line. Let's say you pick the word "Airport", and an image of an "Airplane" to support your chosen word.

Now you have the "Cue Word" from the other actor as "The Airport", and your own keyword from your first line as "The Bar".

The Other Actor: "Meet me at the airport."

You: "I'll be waiting for you at the bar. See you soon."

Now here's where it gets easy.

What we do is to Pair-Link >>> The Airplane with The Bar.

Imagine and Visualize; The bar at the airport has a mini Airplane at its entrance.

So you see the Airplane first at the entrance, and then walk into the bar to meet up with the other person for your next lines.

There you have it. You have memorized your first line by picking two images and connecting them by pair-linking the two together. As soon as you hear "The Airport" from the other actor, you already know your line is coming up soon

You then repeat this process with the rest of your lines.

How to memorize the order of your "Cue Words" together with your own lines in the correct order

So now that you know how to memorize your lines, how do you keep them in order without any confusion?

The most popular and the recommended method is A Memory Palace.

What you need is a memory palace with enough locations to hold your pair links, or your chain links.

With a Memory palace, you can simply mentally walk back to each location to see your saved images.

Create a memory palace based on the amount of locations needed. So if you have 100 lines, you'll need a 100 Locations Memory Palace for all your lines along with the "Cue" words in a pair-link.

The Story or The Journey Method

The story method goes like this. You chain-link all the words following a journey in a story to connect the pairs together. This is a very effective method however I don't recommend it as you may get a broken link that you can't recall which could get you in all sorts of trouble when it comes to memorizing lines!

The Peg palace
Number Shapes Pegs (110 pegs Shaper System)
Number Rhyme Pegs (30 pegs)
Number System Pegs (Major System – 100 pegs)

Number Person Pegs (Dominic System 100 persons)
Alphabet System Pegs (26 Pegs each journey)
Everyday Object Pegs (20 most popular items)
Office Items Pegs (at least 20 office items)

A Grand total of 396 pegs which is enough for a small play.

Peg Palace Method
Because they are numbered, it's easy to follow the path starting from number shapes, then number rhymes, and so on using the Peg palace. The only downside of using the pegs here is that you won't be able to use the same pegs for any other subjects as the pegs will become permanent pegs saved with other permanent information. So when using the peg palace, it's recommended that you always use a memory palace instead.

Read this page from the top again as all of this is already explained in detail so that you can decide which method will work the best for you.

Spaced Repetition With Your Lines – A Must Do.

Make sure to visit your memory palace mentally to see each location with its own images at different time intervals.

For example; Revisit your palace mentally;

- 1 Hour Later
- 6 Hours later
- 12 Hours Later
- A day Later
- A week later
- More if and when needed.

Using these methods with good practice, you'll almost always get your lines correct as you'll know all your Cue Words, and your Cue Images for your lines by heart.

How To Remember Names & Faces

Remembering people's names and faces takes very little effort but will make a great impact in your relationships with other people.

This skill is easily learnable. Anyone can, with a little practice, remember people's names and faces.

Let's dive in and learn how to remember the names & faces of the people you meet.

*** Pay Attention To The Face & Name.**
Decide to remember the name. This is probably the most important part. Decide.

*** Introduce yourself to the person.**

When you introduce yourself, they will then introduce themselves. Make sure to hear the name very clearly. If you didn't then kindly ask for the name again.

*** Make sure to look closely at their face and really take notice of their name.**

It's important that you take in the details of their face and listen attentively.

*** Repeat The Name back To The Person.**

Let's say the name was "Emily". You should instantly repeat the name back to the person (and to yourself) by saying something such as "Nice to meet you Emily".

This alone can help you remember a person's name and face.

The idea of memorizing is to attach as much information as you can to the subject. In this case it's the same. We attach information to the name and the face, so it acts as a clue reminder of what we want to memorize.

*** Start A Conversation.**

Another tip to really cement that name in your brain is to start a conversation and find opportunities to repeat the name during your chat.

This will also be of added value to you when remembering names.

*** Associate The Name With Another Person Of The Same Name by Pair-Linking Both Persons Via An Action.**

Let's say we use the name "Emily" again. If you already know another Emily, then you can imagine the new Emily with the Emily you already know and add an action link between the two to create a memorable mini-story. Make them fight, kiss, push, etc. As long as you can add a little action between the two persons, it will help to ingrain the new face and name in your mind.

*** Give The Person A Location Based On The Name.**

Another way to strengthen the reminder is to think of the person in a location that you'd find her in. Her name is Emily. Now Emily to me sounds like "A Meal". So now I can imagine her having a meal with me at the local restaurant.

This will also help you remember the name very easily as long as you can associate a place to locate the scene.

*** Convert The Name Into A Picture**

Remember what we did before? The name Emily sounded like "A Meal". So I imagine Emily eating a meal.

To find an image for the face, there are 3 basic questions you can ask.

Here are the 3 Questions To Ask Each Time You Need An
Image For A Face.

* What Does The Name Remind You Of?
* What Does The Name Sound Like?
* What Does The Name Look Like?

By answering these questions you should be able to find an
image for any name.

We have found an image for the name Emily as "A Meal". Now
"A Meal" becomes your permanent image for all the names that
are "Emily".

Any name you find an image for can be used over and over on
different people's faces.

*** Pair Link The Name Image To The Face**

Once you have an image for the name, then the method is always
the same. By using your imagination, attach the name image to
the face by an action, and you'll remember it.

In this case, we can imagine "Emily" is eating a meal. And each
time we see Emily, we can immediately see that she is eating a
meal which will immediately remind you of the name.

* Reusable Suffix Visuals For Names

You may sometimes experience some confusion with names. You may meet a person named "Ann", and another named "Anna" or "Gina".

Here is an example of how 'Anna' and 'Gina' might look.

Ann = Hand (assign an action. it might slap the face, draw on the face etc.)

A = Geometric compass (Letter shape that looks like A)

Ann-a

Hand holding a Geometric compass, and draws/uses on the face of Anna.

Gin = Bottle of Gin (Pour over the head, or any spot you choose on the face)

A = Peg (a secondary Letter shape, but you can still use the Geometric compass)

Gin-a

Bottle of Gin poured over the head of Gina while her nose is Pegged with a Peg.

Bottle of Gin poured over the face of Gina while on her nose is a Geometric compass.

in-a = This suggests it's inside of something

So I would choose some large item that the person's head/face/body can fit in.

Let's say we choose "A Huge Empty Glass Bottle" to represent "in-a"

Attach the name image to the suffix image.

G = Ear (Letter shape that looks like an Ear)

Gina = G in-a = Gina is in a Glass Bottle that has a huge Ear.

in-a (inside)

Angel = Angel Wings

Angel-in-a = Angelina is " in a " ** "Glass Bottle" that has "Wings".

So each time you see ina (in-a), the person, or face/head will be placed inside the bottle.

And the image for the name will be either attached, or used as an action applied to the person or the bottle.

The method is to choose an image for each suffix, and reuse them if and when it ends with it.

Try it. You'll have great results.

How To Memorize Images

You can memorize any image, any item, any list and everything else in between as long as you follow the simple method.

It is to attach an image and an action to the item you want to memorize. So this skill will work for all and not just for images.

Let's say you want to memorize a series of images one after another. These images could be pictures, or real everyday items. It makes no difference as these will be recorded in the memory.

Let's say we have 10 photo images, and that we need to memorize it in the correct order.

This is where number shapes and the actions of The Shaper System come in handy as they are already premade in the correct order. However, you can change the actions based on your own liking as they will work the best for you. I will give you the ones I use to memorize images and items, you can then decide to edit to your own.

The Method Of Memorizing Images & Everyday Items.
Let's say you have 10 photos or items. You need to memorize, and recall them in the correct order.

You will need a numbering system to have the images lined up in the correct order.

Here are the pegs with the actions you can use to memorize images in the correct order.

1 = Blow Fire	4 = Knife Cut
2 = Hoover It	5 = Hand Slap
3 = Hop On	6 = Pan Hit

7 = Bomb Explode

8 = Ball Bounce On

9 = Fist Punch

10 = Cook

11 = Drum

12 = Slide

13 = Shoot

14 = Sit

15 = Wheel

16 = Pull

17 = Axe

18 = Sweep

19 = Stamp on

20 = Crawl

21 = Money Rain

22 = Dance

23 = Peck

24 = Alarm

25 = Open

26 = Pour

27 = Dig

28 = Bite

29 = Push

30 = Blow

This list gives you at least 30 images, or everyday items to memorize one by one.

If you wanted to memorize images two at a time, then simply pair-link the two images by an action. That way you can memorize 2 images at a time in the correct order.

The process of memorizing the images

You look at the first image, and choose a part of the image.

You then use a premade image with an action applied to the first photo at the location that you have chosen on the image.

You simply imagine the action is actually happening on the photo itself, or the items.

You then repeat the same process with the rest of the photos or items.

That's how you memorize and recall any image or everyday item, be it a magazine, a shopping list, work list, procedures, and the list goes on. It's one of the easiest one to master and the skill for life that you carry within your mind!

A Secret Language & Password Memory System

I create a daily to do list the night before, ready for the next day. I often write in short codes without using the vowels, such as;

"Pst th lttr". Translates as "Post the letter".

This way I can write and/or make notes very quickly. And the good thing about this is that it is not exactly easy to guess what my to do list is.

I watched the movie "The Imitation Game". Benedict Cumberbatch (one of my Fav actors) acts as Alan Turing who decodes the enigma.

So if this method needs a name then we can perhaps call this as "The EncrypTuring Method"

Since this is a secret language message system, you and friends can message each other using these codes, and have so much fun with it.

All you need is to memorize the Major System codes and create your own secret language, and a password system you can use with ease.

So here is the EncrypTuring Method

The Secret Language Code Of The Numbers.

The Major System is made up of consonant letters that correspond with the number digits from 0-9.

0 - Z-S

1 - T-D-TH

2 - N

3 -M

4 - R

5 - L

6 - CH-SH-JH

7 - Kh, Qh, Gh

8 - F-PH-V

9 - P-B

Now going back to the same example of "Pst Th Lttr"

This translates to "901 1 5114"

These digits are not easy to guess as to what it would mean by anyone who does not know the Major system.

However, it is also not easy to guess even if you do know the Major system as these numbers could also represent different words.

So the idea is to add the Vowels to make the words mean what it's meant to mean for all secret language users.

Let's go back to the same example again;

Pst Th Lttr

901 1 5114

Now let's add the Vowels.

9o01 1he 5e11e4

Notice now a consonant "h" stands out as it is not a vowel. It's up to you to use "h" or simply use "1" as "th".

The other consonants such as "w, y, x" that you may use where necessary with either symbols or as they are. I use "?" as "w", and use "y, and x" as they are.

The easiest way is to simply use the missing consonants to make up the word to create your own secret language.

Now this doesn't have to be the usual Major system codes, you can in fact change the Letters to some other consonants that you and the other/s person/s want to use as your own secret language.

Some of the shortcuts you can use

At: @

Why: ?

Why-Not: ?2o1

What: ?1

Where: ?4

How: h?

Which: ?6

When: ?2

Who: ?h

You: u, or U

Hi: h or H

Hello: hE55o

And: &

Number: # (example: 1pm: #1-93 or 9am: #9-a3)

Yes: y0

No: 2o

OK: o7

See: < (looks like an eye looking to the right)

See you: <U

Would: w1 (Wood: woO1)

Could: c1

Will: ?55

Sorry: 04y

Thank you: 1a27u.   Tonight: 1o2iy1

Today: 1o1aY   Later: 5a14. OR 5a1E4.

Tomorrow: 1o3r?

So this can be used as a secret language code for messaging.

Password System

As easy as it gets, this little system can also be used for setting up and remembering passwords with a single word/image.

Simply follow the same procedure, but use it as a password instead!

Hope you have lots of fun with it.

See if you can translate this code into words? i-5o8e 32e3o2i70.

Effective Learning Methods With Mnemonics

Let's say that you have 5 major points, and under each point, there are multiple things to memorize.

Do these actions below, you can then use spaced repetition and you should be able to memorize it all that will stay with you for a long time, perhaps months and years.

First, you have to know what each subject and key point mean. Read each key point word for word a few times and learn what they all mean in depth.

See if you can summarize all the key points in your own words as if you are teaching it to someone else. Try it a few times. If you get stuck, then learn a little more, and then summarize again until you do know them well enough.

Once you can summarize it, see if you can give some examples of one or two facts about it. Again do this as if you are teaching it to a person. A real person is even better.

Record your voice with a gadget if you have one while you summarize it. Once you press the record button, just relax, and forget that it's there. And carry on talking.

Now it's time to ask questions. Create a question for each key point you summarized, and then answer it. Perhaps create another question if you have the need for it. The more the better. Use "What, Why, How" in your questions, so it cannot be answered with a yes or a no.

Now that you have the mind-map, and you know what each key point means very well, you can then take them into your long term memory using a memory palace.

In your Memory palace; If you have 5 Major points, then create 5 rooms.

In your first room, for the first Major Point/Subject, if you have 5 key points that belong to it, then you need 5 locations around that room that will belong to that Major Key point.

Find an image for each key point, in this case you need 5 images for the first room.

Place the images around the room at those 5 locations. Perhaps make the image do something with an item at that location. This will strengthen it even further as it would act as a Recall-Trigger. The locations and the items at the locations will trigger what you have placed there.

Once you place the images, then practice visualizing them all in your mind, seeing each item at their own location and what they do at the location. Better if you go clockwise, so you are not crossing in a zig-zag.

If you are confident with the first room, meaning you have memorized them all, then repeat this same procedure for the rest of the rooms.

Take a break every 30 minutes or so, let your mind relax.

Use spaced repetitions at timed intervals

So review it later on that evening, next day, a week later, and a few weeks later. And you should be able to remember them all for a long time to come if not a lifetime!

How To Memorize Dates & Appointments

When you want to memorize numbers for dates and appointments, this simple Mnemonic Clock I have designed will be your best friend. Try it and see how well it works for you.

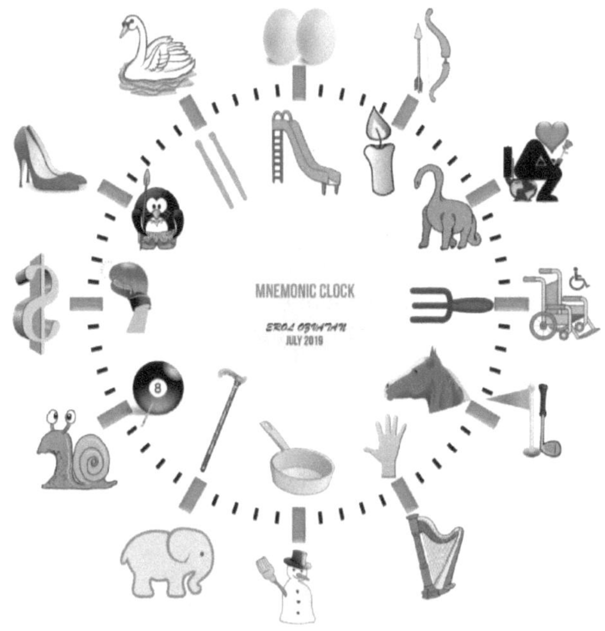

How To Use The Mnemonic Clock

Let's say that you are picking up your aged Mother at 09:15 am.

The inner circle of the clock has the images from 1-12. The outer circle has the images from 13 - 00. The last two Eggs represents 00 as the clock reset itself at the 24th hour.

So with this appointment of you collecting your Mother at 09.15,
09 = Boxer's Glove with A Right Hook Punch
15 = Wheelchair.
Location = Mother's House Door or Living Room.

So the mini-story link could be;
You are at the house door to pick her up, the door opens your Mother Punches you with a Right Hook wearing a Huge Boxer' Glove, While sitting on the Wheelchair

Unless of course you want to use it the other way; Mother being punched while she is sitting on the wheelchair. It's your world.

Make it more vivid and more memorable, by making up a story why she's just punched you with a boxing glove, and why she'd be sitting on that wheelchair. Make it as funny as you can possibly make it

As for the second appointment at 09.43
You'd be "Punching" the "Horse with a Fork stuck in its head", at the location you have the meeting or the appointment.

Punching = 09
The Horse With a Fork Stuck (or Stabbed) in its head = 43

Let's do some more examples;

If another appointment was at 11.51, at the doctors.

You'd see yourself playing Drums (11)

on the Doctor himself at his/her room (loci)

Holding (5)

A Candle (1)

If another appointment was at 06.04, at the bank.

You'd see the receptionist Greeting you at the bank (Loci)

offering you a "Fried (06)"

Horse-Head (04)"

And as usual, to make it more memorable, you'd create an episodic reasoning, make it as funny as you can, that usually is good enough for instant recall.

How To Memorize Conversations

If you want to memorize some key information on the fly, then I recommend you use the body method. It is very useful.

You can also use any other object that is in front of you or around you. Such as a Car can be a palace on the fly, a Chair can be one, a desk can be used, an animal such as a Dog can be another. Use whatever you can see to quickly create a few spots on the objects to store the "Key Points/Words" you choose at the time of the conversation.

Another method is to use the surroundings of the location you are at, and use the Chain-Link Pairing Method. So once you choose the Key-Word/s of the conversation, Chain-Link them by pairing them together, and add that to your surroundings. While doing so, you can also use Number shapes to follow the order of the conversation, and to help you make the links

Here is an example;

Persons name is Gino | Keyword: Bottle Of Gin (o)
He works at the local book-shop | Keyword: Book
He has 2 Daughters | Keywords: Swan + Kids
The live in Minnesota | Keyword: Mini-Soda Drink or a small Can Of Soda

Start with Gino holding a Bottle Of Gin, and Pouring it over a Giant Book as big as him which is next to him. Notice that a magic wand is printed on the cover of the book, this is the number shape for 1. *You have paired Two Keywords here.*

You then see a big Swan, and on it is 2 kids. Kids picks up the giant book, and Pours a Mini-Soda Can over the book, it's wet and dripping soda.

Now you have paired the next 2 keywords.

Basically it's a chain-link in pairs that happens faster than you read this above.

Bottle Gin Poured Over The Book, Kids Pick it up, and Pours a miniature Soda over the book.

The magic wand and the swan represents the order of the links. So you know what was said first and second and so on.

Number shapes can also be used to create links when used with its actions

Gino is Holding a Magic Wand, and makes a Bottle of Gin appear. This is the action of the magic wand which represent the digit 1.

So by using the actions of the number shapes, you can create the links instantly because you'd already know the actions memorized as part of your training.

Part 6

Practice Apps To Start Your Training

- The Shaper System Images
- Memory Palace Desktop App
- Numbers Memory Practice Desktop App
- Binary Numbers Practice Desktop App
- Playing cards Practice Desktop App
- The Shaper System "Spreadsheet"

Part 6
Practice Apps To Start Your Training

Download both versions of The Shaper System FOR FREE! on paolist.com

Files and License Rights

The full version of The Shaper System consists of the following files from the "paolist.com" for FREE download.

The Shaper System Images

- All 100 Number-To-Shape Images
- All 100 Number-To-Real Pictures
- All 26 English Alphabet-Letter-Shape To Peg-Images
- All 100 Memory Palace Background Images.
- All 100 Sample Persons To Change With Your Own.

Memory Palace Desktop App

100 stops journey, with 100 background images, specifically chosen for the memory palace. Expandable to 500 Locations.

The app will load the images of the shaper palace one by one by for you to memorize your palace in the correct order.

Numbers Memory Practice Desktop App

This is the desktop app with the following functions;

- Ability to change every single image with your own to have the final system of your own
- Loads the Shaper images for each two digit combination.
- Loads Object + Object as a pair, so you can practice your; "OO": Object paired with the next Object by its Action.
- Loads Person + Objects as a pair, so you can practice

your; "PA": Person paired with the next Object by its Action.

- Loads The Shaper Palace that consists of 100 background scenes.

Binary Numbers Practice Desktop App

This is the desktop app with the following functions;

* Ability to change every single image with your own to have the final system of your own

* Loads the Shaper images for each binary combination.

* Loads Object + Object as a pair, so you can practice your; "OO": Object paired with the next Object by its Action

* Loads Person + Objects as a pair, so you can practice your; "PA": Person paired with the next Object by its Action.

* Loads The Shaper Palace that consists of 100 background scenes.

Playing cards Practice Desktop App

This is the desktop app with the following functions;

- Ability to change every single image with your own to have the final system of your own!
  * Loads the Shaper images for each two card combination.
- Loads Object + Object as a pair, so you can practice your; "OO": Object paired with the next Object by its Action.
  Loads Person + Objects as a pair, so you can practice your
- "PA": Person paired with the next Object by its Action.
- Loads The Shaper Palace that consists of 100 background scenes.

The Shaper System "Spreadsheet"

With All 100 Persons Actions Objects, and more..

This spreadsheet is a self explanatory - ready to use out of the box with the shaper system.

It's specifically designed to teach and help you practice all the sections of the whole shaper system.
It's also editable so you can edit and/or change any of the persons, actions, and the rest of the fields to organize it into your own system.

Practice | Practice | Practice

Once you master this spreadsheet, apply all the principles with at least 1 hour practice a day, and you'll be on your way to memorize 100s of digits easily. This will help you in many ways during your life as numbers are in almost every part of our everyday life.

Have Fun!

The Certificate Of Completion Free PSD Design
I have provided the PSD Photoshop File so you can edit and use it if you teach and want to certify your students.

The Shaper System Downloads & Licence Rights

Use and Edit For Personal - **YES.**

Distribute For Non-Profit **- YES - Unedited.**

Teach For Non-Profit Using The Files **- YES - Unedited.**

Add or edit or remove images For Personal Use- **YES.**

Can be used as web or e-zine content - **YES** - With Written Permission.

For all enquiries;

Contact Erol Ozvatan

https://paolist.com

Conclusion

With regular study and practice, the techniques you have learned in this book will help you to develop not only an excellent memory but increased mental stamina and brainpower!

With focus and dedication, there will be no limit to what you can achieve!

I hope you have enjoyed this journey to developing a trained brain.

The key is practice. Read, Learn, Prepare, and Practice as much as you can.

And don't forget to have fun! It'll be worth it!

About The Author

Hello. My name is "Erol Özvatan". I was born in 1969 in Turkey in the beautiful city of Izmir. Since I was 18 years old, most of my life has been spent in England and also in many other countries of the world for visits, business, commerce, research and education. For the past twelve years, I have done extensive high level research on the brain, logic and memory development. I have learned and practiced my training materials from the world's most recognized memory experts. The most famous of which are Dominic O'Brien, Tony Buzan, Ed Cooke, Kevin Trudeau, Ron White, Harry Lorayne, from the oldest to the newest - and studied and learned each of their systems. I have read 20 memory books from 20 different authors. After that, I studied 11 different courses and got my certificates of achievement for Memory and its usage areas via Udemy. I learned many different systems and methods and I practiced and experimented.

To gain a deeper understanding of how memory works, I undertook training and completed the "Memory and Psychology" course from the Wesleyan University Department of Psychology to further enrich my knowledge about memory, brain, and psychological relationships.

I wanted to innovate, improve, and further develop an existing system taught in memory development training. My aim was to make it simple to understand, simple to prepare, and fairly simple to apply. And by further developing this system, I have established an improved version of the number shape system in January 2018 - "The Shaper System ©", which is a type of association system utilizing a Number-To-Image Generator.

I presented this system in the world's most visited Memory Forum - **The Art Of Memory Forum**. And to my surprise It attracted a lot more attention than I ever thought it would. It received 8800 impressions, a huge amount of comments with 1000s of lines of text.

There was a lot of talk about how useful it would be as a new system and how it can be used with existing systems. I started to get a lot of questions about the subject and Emails from people from various countries of the world. There were also those who contacted me on Facebook and wanted to study the system. And I still receive a huge amount of emails, messages in pm on the forum, and through Facebook.

In order to better understand the impact rate of this system, I participated in Online Memory competitions to test and reinforce myself. In the third season contest, I finished third in a 10-person cluster. In the fourth season, I went up a division, and Won my division . I managed to take part in the Third League in the next season, and I managed to finish second after very tough matches.

My current place is the 2nd league in the online Memory league. And I still participate in competitions whenever I have time.

My main goal here was to better learn how useful this system was, and I saw that even a 50-year-old person as myself was effective enough to get some decent results in competitions.

Here are my personal best performances in competitions and in training;

- Memorize pictures in the correct order – 30 pictures 21 seconds.
- Memorize words in the correct order – 30 words in 60 seconds
- Names and Faces – 21 Names and faces in 60 seconds
- One Deck of Playing Cards – 52 Cards in 120 seconds
- Memorize the number digits in order – 67 numbers in 57 seconds.

You'll also find me on "**The Art Of Memory Forum**", and my name under "Erol Ozvatan" on "**The Memory Techniques Wiki**" with the system and methods I developed.

I am proud to see my name in the "**Famous mnemonist**" page. I am very proud to be in **The Memory Techniques Wiki** where I share all my methods and useful information related to memory. It's a great honor to see my name next to the Memory Masters I have learned a lot from!

The Shaper System Full Package Is A Free Download For All Memory Improvement Enthusiasts from paolist.com.

The full shaper system from the start to its final stage took around 2 years of preparation, trial and error, and corrections, and finally it's ready to use out of the box.

All I want in return is that you say "**Thank you**". That would be my **good prayer** from you, that I have helped another person towards achieving their goal.

I wish you all the best in developing a powerful memory.

Erol Ozvatan

9 7 9 8 7 1 4 6 2 7 4 5 3